CW00516311

Diane Valerie
Burgess

THE ROADS WE TRAVEL

novum ⬟ pro

www.novum-publishing.co.uk

© 2023 novum publishing

ISBN 978-3-99131-927-6
Editing: Charlotte Middleton
Cover photo:
Yuliya Baturina I Dreamstime.com
Cover design, layout & typesetting:
novum publishing

www.novum-publishing.co.uk

All rights of distribution,
including via film, radio, and television,
photomechanical reproduction,
audio storage media, electronic data
storage media, and the reprinting of
portions of text, are reserved.

Printed in the European Union on
environmentally friendly, chlorine- and
acid-free paper.

Climate neutral
Print product
ClimatePartner.com/16547-2201-1002

With this book I would like to support
the Soi Dog Foundation.

The Rain Beats a Lullaby

I could not sleep,
Then the storm came in.
It made me feel the most serene,
I had ever been.

The lullaby
The rain beat,
Had sung me gently
Off to sleep.

I slept soundly
As lightning lit the sky,
And thunder clouds
Rolled slowly by.

When I awoke
To birdsong
The stirring storm
Had long since gone.

The air was fresh,
The sky was clear
No memory for most,
That a storm was here;

But each night I pray
For the stormy rain,
So I can sleep peacefully
Once again.

Another Piece of Childhood Gone

There used to be an old house on the corner,
Where us young kids would go and hang around.
They demolished it, ten years ago,
Because it was falling down.
And the school where I spent my formative years –
Some bad, but mostly good –
Was closed down when the cash ran out,
And is now all boarded up.
Why is it, as we get older,
And we want to reminisce,
The things that were once major in our lives –
The things we never thought we'd miss –
Are the things we long to see again
Since our lives have now moved on,
But they're now just passages written in time,
And another piece of childhood gone.
How I wish I could ride the dirt again,
Where the big superstore now stands.
Riding freely on my bike,
Through tough and gritty lands.
And the old man who used to live at the top of the hill,
Whom we affectionately called Uncle John,
Moved 'upstairs' to Our Lord, a long time ago,
Yet another piece of childhood gone.
I guess that's why we have memories,
They're what tie our years together,
And like our lives, nothing stays the same,
And nothing lasts forever.
Like the seasons come and go,
Things they have to move on,
But it's always affecting to see another
Piece of childhood gone.

As I watch the young kids playing now,
I wonder if they realise
That in just thirty years or so,
This place they won't recognise,
And I wonder if it will make them see
How quickly things move on,
And make them feel sad, like I do now,
At another piece of childhood gone.
I only wish they knew it now,
Before it's a piece of childhood gone.

Face Value

I'd only ever 'heard' the phrase –
A face 'etched with pain' – before,
But as I look into your eyes,
I now know what it means for sure.

It tells a whole story,
In just a few sad lines.
I guess no matter what you try to hide,
The face betrays the soul sometimes.

I don't normally take
Anything I see at face value,
But your face is testament
To all that you have been through.

Every scar and every line
Tells of how your soul was broken,
It recounts a heart-breaking tale,
Without a single word being spoken.

Every hurt and every loss,
Has left a visible trace.
A track of tears and despair,
Upon your weary face.

Sometimes we choose not to look,
Because we don't want to see,
But how can you ignore an open book,
Displayed so tragically.

The Kitten and the Rain

The kitten sits on the window ledge,
Her nose pressed to the windowpane.
At first, fascination, then utter consternation
To catch the falling rain.
As she watches and she tries
She turns her head
From side to side
And up and down –
She's mystified!

She's sure she caught
That last one,
But when she looks
It has gone!
And as each new
Raindrop falls
She ties herself in knots
Trying to catch them all.

She runs the wood and spies to chase,
But all her efforts seem to fail,
And she jumps and arches her back
When the soft rain turns to hail.
In the end
She gives up;
She's not impressed,
She's had enough.

She's more than vexed
With this game,
So she slinks off
With her back to the rain.
But then she's not one
To walk away
When there's actually 'quite'
A fun game to play.

So she jumps on the table beside the window ledge,
Peers around and fixes her eyes.
She's determined to catch a raindrop
With the element of surprise!
And so the game continues
And her ambition carries on.
She knows she's sure to be the winner,
When the rain stops and is all gone.

She Walks With the Wolves

She walks with the wolves,
And her voice is the wind across the plain.
She sleeps beside the lion
And with eagles soars o'er the mountain range.
She is the clean, fresh air,
The pure water of the falls.
She is the guardian of nature,
Walking with the wolves.
She cups her hands and takes a sip of water
From the cool, crystal stream,
And it reflects her transcendent beauty
That seldom few have seen.
The lion – her protector – walks on ahead,
She is part of his pride,
And the white wolf from the northern country
Never leaves her side.
She oversees the storm
As it threatens in the sky.
She burnishes the lightning
And herds the thunder clouds as they roll by.
She walks barefoot from one landscape to the next,
And as the early morning calls
She rouses the beast;
Her soft call awakens the flowers
As she walks with the wolves.
She runs her hand thru' the willow,
Walks kindly thru' the reeds.
Her gentle touch nurtures the land
And gives the nourishment it needs.
Be it the lowlands, plain or snowy woodland,
She is the keeper of it all.
The tender custodian who brings the light
As she walks with the wolves.

I Just Haven't Found One Yet

I want to fight for something,
I'm just not sure what.
People say I'm a 'rebel without a cause'
But I'm really not.

The whole world over,
There are fights being lost and won.
Some use their voice or a pen
Whilst others use a knife, a gun.

There are heroes and cowards,
Dreamers and fools.
Some will go by the book,
Whilst others break the rules.

Some will make the headlines,
Others battle silently,
But they all have a goal in sight
And I want that for me!

So like a stranger is a friend
That you've just never met,
I'm not a 'rebel without a cause' –
I just haven't found one yet.

No-one Else to Talk to

The girl sits on the shoreline, talking to herself,
People pass her by, knowing she's lost and confused,
But their compassion doesn't stretch to a girl who's slightly crazy,
And they've seen her so many times, to them she is old news.
The pastor always says a prayer, at church for her on Sunday,
And they all nod their heads as they say Amen,
But the vulnerable girl he asked them
to give help and strength to,
Never runs thru' their minds again.
If they saw somebody fall down,
They'd pick them up and take them home,
But they won't even approach the girl
Who sits talking, on her own.
They don't understand her reasons –
And they'd be ashamed if they knew –
That she is only talking to herself
Because there's no-one else to talk to.
One day the girl's not on the shoreline,
No-one knows where she has gone –
And nobody questions it –
Not a single one,
And after a few days
It's like she didn't exist.
They're not concerned that she is gone
And she will not be missed.
No-one had seen her fall down,
There was no-one to pick her up.
No-one ever looked for her
Because no-one cared enough,
And when by chance somebody found her on the rocks
It was clear the darkness had won through.
But maybe things would have been different,
If she'd had someone to talk to.

Goodbye to a Friend

Taking in one last look of every room,
Memories come fast, emotions stir inside.
We've lived here for almost twenty years,
And it's hard to say goodbye.

I know it's only bricks and mortar
But I feel like I'm losing a friend.
I run my hand over the outdated wallpaper,
Remembering when the pattern was all the trend.

I try to tell myself 'It's just a house,'
The kids are now all grown,
But I remember so fondly
This was once our family home.

It was our shelter in the storms of life,
Our stability when life got crazy.
The ups, the downs, the in-betweens,
It was the beating heart that never ceased to amaze me.

I know I can take the memories with me,
But it will always be here they were made.
There'll always be a little part of 'us' left behind,
Steeped in the foundations that our family laid.

There are memories etched in every room,
Of the good times and the bad.
This house shared our dreams and aspirations,
Witness to every precious moment that we had.

Then I hear my husband come into the room,
It's already time for us to go.
I notice his eyes are red – he's been crying too –
But he wouldn't want me to know.

I pull the front door shut,
Lock it for the very last time,
Knowing this place will always hold
The story that was mine.

I whisper 'You have a new family,
Make special memories with them.
Keep them safe from the storms like you did for us,
I'll remember you always, my dear friend.'

The True Heart of Her Affection

She sits on the wooden stool,
Drinking in the bar.
She takes her time with her drink,
The few pounds she has left won't get her far.

She had the offer of 'free' drinks all night,
Lots of lonely men with cash to spend,
But she's far from that kind of girl,
Knowing how they would expect the night to end.

The bar keeper calls last orders,
She heads outside into the cool air,
Pulls her coat around her, lights a cigarette,
And ties back her tousled hair.

Walking quickly her shoes clip the pavement,
And soon, the neons dim.
She doesn't have much further to go
Until she's back home with him.

She ignores the whooping and hollering
Coming from the passing cars,
She knows it's just good-natured high spirits
Continuing on from the emptying bars.

She stubs out her cigarette on a wall –
Making sure it's out – she flicks it into a bin.
Feeling excited, her home is close
And she admits tonight, she's felt lost without him.

He hadn't wanted her to go out tonight,
And as she gets closer to her front door
She sees his silhouette through the glass,
She missed him, but he missed her more.

She pulls her door keys from her pocket,
The pink fluffy ball attached bobs as she slips in the keys,
And even though she can see him patiently waiting,
She still shouts 'Honey, it's only me.'

Although she likes to spend some time in the bar,
It's coming home that she likes more,
And the reason is there to greet her
As she walks through the door.

He's always happy to see her home,
And tonight is no exception.
The boy in her life – her new little lab puppy,
The 'true heart of her affection'.

Dreamcatcher

Come, dreams,
Come and explore this world of mine,
Created on the reservation by gifted hands,
Expressive patterns of intricate twine.

Come, dreams,
You know that I will not ignore you.
If you are of good nature, then you I will gently hold,
And if you're not, the sun awaits you.

I will sway easily in the open window's breeze,
For I am the guardian above the bed,
And the fresh air that encircles me
Is from the feathers, where I take my every breath.

Come, dreams,
Come and explore my exquisite web of braid,
Come a little closer,
See of what I'm made.

Are you mesmerised by my beads –
Bad dreams come and I'll guide you through
Straight into the sun's golden rays –
It's been waiting for you.

Sweet dreams,
Let us come together.
Come forth and bring your happiness,
Fly upon the feather.

I am the dreamcatcher,
I will hold the dreams that 'calm and soothe',
So sleep, sleep soundly,
For I am here to protect you.

One step ahead of two steps back

You can ask him where he was yesterday
Or the day before,
But he'll tell you that he can't remember,
That he's not really sure.

It might not be the answer
That you expect,
But he'll say it's not where he's been that matters,
It's where he's going next.

He'll tell you he's been here and there,
And how many miles he has covered,
He doesn't care to remember names
When there's so much to be discovered.

Every day, every place there's something new,
And the only thing he's sure of is this –
His mind's so full of incredible new things,
It doesn't matter where he is.

You can ask him where he's going tomorrow
And the day after that,
And he'll tell you it's another day of revelation,
That's two steps ahead of one step back.

A bookcase of diaries

Spanning twenty years or more.
She dates and places each one carefully as she finishes it,
But never reads the ones before.

For years they have sat there,
Only moved so she can dust.
The written history of her life hidden away
On every page of every book.

She knows if she took a look – at any book –
There would be a memory that would cause her upset,
And she doesn't want to remember all the things
She's tried so hard to forget.

Her friends question her reasons
For filling in a new diary every year,
If she doesn't read them,
What use are they to her?

She'll say she writes down all the things
that happen in her life,
The good, the bad and all the trials that she's faced,
But for her, it's more an 'emblem of survival'
That sits in that bookcase.

Last moments

It was the last thing I wanted to say to you,
But I knew it's what you wanted to hear
And I didn't want your last moments
To be filled with anxiety and fear.

I just hope you couldn't feel
My poor scared and trembling heart
Because I knew he who brought us together
Was about to tear us apart.

I gently whispered to you not to worry –
We'd all be okay,
But I knew deep down you understood
I just wanted you to stay.

I just wish we could have talked to each other at the end,
But that wasn't to be.
I could whisper to you
But you couldn't talk to me.

I gently stroked your face and kissed you
Like you used to do to reassure me when I was a kid.
I would've given everything for you to do it back to me,
But you never did.

Even in those last few moments
I somehow held back my tears,
And even after you'd gone,
Just in case you could still hear.

It's been almost a year now,
And there hasn't been a minute
That this harsh world has warmed up for me,
It's so cold without your heartbeat in it.

Regret becomes the natural enemy,
When you lose someone.
All the things you wish you had said,
Before they were gone.

I have to be honest, those last few moments,
I fear are a memory that will last forever,
And you're probably shouting at me right now
To focus on all the good times we shared together.

I've tried to do that –
But those sweet memories make me cry –
Because like for everyone, the hardest one
Is at the end you have to say goodbye.

Good Question

One day – after school – my little boy,
Looking puzzled, ran up to me.
He told me, his teacher had said
'There are animals in every corner of the world,'
And he said he wasn't sure how that could be.
I asked what had confused him –
What it was he didn't understand,
He said 'How can the world have corners,
When the earth is round?'
Luckily before I got chance to explain,
He added that the teacher had also said
That there are unidentified places and creatures
That we haven't discovered yet!
'I don't understand it, mommy,
If there're places we've never been,
How can we know there are animals there
That we've never seen?'
I struggled to formulate a simple answer,
When I did, he said he still wasn't sure,
Then he saw his friend and decided to go and talk cars,
And thankfully never asked me anything more.
Don't get me wrong, I'm proud of my bright little boy,
Whose curiosity never ceases to amaze me,
And I know there are many more questions to come
That will no doubt drive me crazy.
So, I've decided when he asks,
'Mommy, where do babies come from?'
I'll definitely have an answer for that,
And I'll say 'Go and ask your daddy, son.'

Mom

As the early morning rain falls against my window
With its every beat I'll be reminded of you,
Because it's resonating melody sounds
like your beautiful heartbeat,
That I would always take comfort in lying next to.

There will be no anguish, no fear,
When the storms of life will come,
Because I'll feel your loving arms around me,
Protecting me the way you've always done.

In the soft, temperate breeze, I'll hear your voice,
The sweet lullaby you used to sing,
And I'll hear your words of wisdom to safely guide me,
Gently whispered in the wind.

I'll hear your laughter in the thunder,
See your footprints in the snow.
Your sweet, gentle spirit in every butterfly,
Your pure beauty in every rose.

Behind every dark and stirring storm
Always follows the sun,
But not even its radiance can light up this world
As much as you did – my best friend – my precious Mom.

Angel From the Wrong Side of the Tracks

Like white petals from a rose sent from heaven,
Snow.
Falling gently,
Then cascading
Dark horizon
Sunlight fading
Gives a cold warm glow
Snow.

Ethereal white spirit,
Swings her cloak of white.
She dusts the air and covers the earth,
And makes the dark seem light.
She can be so barbed and treacherous – but so beautiful,
Snow.
So pure, so fragile
So infinitely breath-taking.

So harsh, so cruel,
So hard and soul-breaking.
She's the angel that people love to see,
But after a while want her to go,
Snow.
She scatters the delicate snowflake – so unique
She stitches each of them one by one,
But as they fall to the earth, then upon each other,
That frail elegance is soon gone.

Angel from the wrong side of the tracks,
Snow.
She bejewels the tree with her angel dust
That melts with just a single touch.
The magic is fleeting – a momentary pause,
But this beauty is also harsh and raw,
And most are pleased to see her go,
Snow.

But if you look behind the bitter and the bleak,
Behold the intricate story she has told.
In an unrelenting climate,
She weaves magic into the cold.

Beauty is the Beast (A Cat's Tale)

Away in the distance
A soulful cry.
A sleek black silhouette
Sweeps a burnt orange sky.

A tremble runs through
Those who hear his call,
Strong and tenacious,
Yet the most lonesome of all.

As he stalks deep into the night,
He's a beast from the wild.
But as dusk turns into dawn,
He's the best friend of a small child.

The dark and powerful hunter
Now casts a soft, gentle shadow instead.
The haunting cry, now a gentle purr
As he lies snuggled on the bed.

You'll wonder what he's thinking
As you fall into those corn-golden eyes,
But if you knew the half of it,
It would still leave you mystified.

The next minute the familiar is gone again,
But he's hidden in plain sight.
Not here, not there, but everywhere,
Slinking off into the night.

A Flicker of the Light That Once Brightly Burned

A Poem About Dementia

Sometimes it's like that he's not there,
Almost as if he cannot see,
And I can feel his pain as he tries to remember
Who he is to me.

His eyes they seem so dark now,
Where once they burned so bright.
It's as if someone has stolen him
And turned out the light.

And when I think that I've really lost him,
And he'll never, ever return,
There will be a flicker
Of the light that once brightly burned.

For a time it brushes away my sadness,
When he does recall,
And that memory becomes more precious,
Because that's the greatest gift of all.

I'll treasure those few moments,
When he talks freely of the past,
And I'll lock them safely in my heart,
Because I know that they won't last.

He's still the man I fell in love with –
I know he's changed, but he'll always be
The man I share great memories with,
The man who still lights the flame that burns in me.

I'll keep those beautiful memories for both of us,
So they will never die,
Because each time that I lose a little bit more of him,
It seems every day is another goodbye.

Our love is on strong foundations,
And it's never been broken yet,
So I will be his memories
For the times he will forget.

I'm not saying that it's easy,
But real hope has returned,
And I'll be there to nurture that flicker
Of the light that once brightly burned.

Bare Walls

All of your photographs
That I should have on the wall
Are locked away with the memories,
Inside my old desk drawer.

I have them close to me,
They're an open – but closed – book.
I miss you so much
I'm too afraid to look.

The walls are bare, to stop my soul from breaking,
My heart is already broken in two.
What would be the point of documenting
How much I so desperately miss you.

The walls are bare
To keep my spirit from dying.
It's not that I don't want to remember,
I'm just so afraid of trying.

I don't want precious memories to remind me,
Like other people do,
Because all the happy memories I ever had,
I shared only with you.

I guess I could have paintings,
But there'd be no point at all,
Because they have stories of their own
And I've grown accustomed to bare walls.

Troublemaker

Just because I'm seen as a troublemaker,
Doesn't mean what I say is wrong.
It doesn't make my argument worth any less
Just because I push it a little strong.

I'm a fighter for justice,
Although I know I come across a little too emphatic.
It's true I like to shake things up
And I'm not the most diplomatic.

I'm outspoken – I say what has to be said,
Occasionally I'm a risk taker.
So people are often of the opinion
That I'm a troublemaker.

Sometimes words are the only weapon
And it can easily get out of hand.
When frustration leads to an anger
The other side neglect to understand.

I stand for every one
Who's fed up of banging their heads on a wall,
Against those who claim they understand,
But have no idea at all.

So sometimes you have to stir the hornets' nest
If you're to get justice properly served,
And if that makes me a troublemaker,
Well then, perhaps it's a label well deserved.

Nothing to Anyone

He sits in the corner of the time-worn cupboard,
His gloved hands almost touching the floor.
A red-and-blue striped playsuit, a fixed wooden smile,
Although deep inside he isn't smiling any more.
Next to him sits an old-fashioned typewriter,
Most of the keys on its keyboard have fallen out.
Just like him, it's no longer useful to anybody,
He feels it sums up what his life is all about.

A beautiful past, so loved in his time,
But now, like the varnish on his face – it's all faded away.
Left in the cupboard, just an old piece of wood,
He sadly knows he's nothing to anyone today.
Beside the typewriter is an aged woven blanket,
With more patches and stitches than weave.
Just another discarded, lost and unloved thing,
That once gave so much comfort – but today nobody needs.

He sits in the corner of the once smart wooden cupboard,
His hands almost touching the floor.
Tear-stained wood of a toy once so loved,
Who is now nothing to anyone any more.
Bewildered and forgotten – the only time they see someone
Is when another outworn, dated something is thrown in.
He still hopes that he will be found and loved again,
But right now – if he had a heart –
it would be breaking inside him.

Super-duper Clever Cat Play Station

Cats are just like children
When it comes to Christmas time,
And parents will always be parents
When it comes to getting the best gift they can find.

So when I saw the advertisement,
I ordered it without hesitation –
The most amazing of them all –
The super-duper clever cat play station.

I had been hypnotised and mesmerised
By the colourful feathers, mice and balls
That raced up and down a flood-lit track
And for the cleverest cats of all.

So much more than just a toy,
An engineering revelation.
A dream, a joy, the best you can get
a super-duper cat sensation.

It arrived on Christmas Eve,
The box said – just ten minutes to put together,
It took me three hours – so I don't know about the cats,
It's the owners who need to be clever!

But finally when it was finished,
I looked proudly at the feline dream I'd created,
And I'm not sure whether it was the excitement – or the wine
But I was feeling pretty elated.

Quietly I played with that toy
For the rest of the night.
Well, it is the cat owner's 'responsibility'
To check it's put together right!

Then Christmas Day was here
And she walked into the room,
I was so excited,
I couldn't wait to see the happiness on her face,
She was sure to be delighted.

I stood there and held my breath,
I could hardly contain the feeling inside
As she looked at what I had built for her,
My chest bursting with pride.

She walked from one side to the other,
But she wasn't looking too impressed.
She nonchalantly flicked a ball with her paw,
Then ignored the rest.

I sat down, deflated,
I was truly disappointed – but maybe,
Although I thought I bought it for her –
Perhaps I really bought it for me.

All this proves what I've known all along,
That she's independently intelligent – as ever,
And she didn't need a new-fangled toy
To prove that she was clever.

She had sort of acknowledged my efforts –
Well, as much as an unimpressed cat can –
So I went to tell her 'Merry Christmas',
Goodwill to feline and to man.

Then I saw all was not lost,
There was a part of the gift she was interested in,
And it's where I found her, fast asleep,
In the box that it came in!

No Experience Required

You write so beautifully of love,
But say you've never been shown it.
So how do you get it all so right
If you've never known it?

The euphoria of that first kiss,
The excitement and the fear.
I'm sure you must have lived it,
Because the words are so honest, the emotions so clear.

The first moment you hold each other,
Of not wanting to let go.
Tell me how you 'get' all of this,
If you really don't know.

You speak of that first argument,
Where the words cut you like a knife
And the moment you first realise she's the one
You want to be with for life.

You write so poetically
Of what being in love brings.
So it's hard to believe
You've never experienced those things.

As I read your words I can feel the butterflies
Rising in my chest – they fly –
And I long to feel the love you express
And it brings tears to my eyes.

You epitomise the palpable fear of losing that someone
Who makes your life complete.
I can feel the empathy and the joy
Amongst the words, so bitter sweet.

You write of hearts and roses,
Ask if they're really enough.
I can feel the anxiety between each line
As you grieve the fragility of love.

You say you've never been in love,
Felt wanted or desired,
That you just write of what you long for,
No experience required.

The dream of meeting that soulmate,
And there is nothing more admired
Than the way you choose your words so well
That proves 'no experience required'.

Until You're Lost No More

I promise I won't stop looking for you
Until the day you're found,
I said I'd always keep you safe,
But now I see I've let you down.
I know you must be somewhere,
I just don't know where for sure,
But I will keep looking for you
Until you're lost no more.
I only wish I'd kept you safe,
Then you might still be here.
I wonder was it something that I did
That made you disappear.
Even if it takes forever,
And whatever lies in store,
I'll climb every mountain and follow every road
Until you're lost no more.
No matter where it takes me,
Even if each road leads to nowhere,
I will walk them to their end,
To make sure that you're not there.
Nothing will stop me
Even when my time is through
'Cause there is nothing in this world
That will stop me finding you.
There'll be no obstacles to faze me,
Of that you can be sure.
I'm going to follow every path
Until you're lost no more.
I'll open every door that's locked
Until you're lost no more.

Ashes to Dust

The curtains are almost fully drawn,
But through the small gap slips a ray of sunlight.
An almost perfect, grey sparkling, dusty line,
Like a lighthouse lamp's beam guiding ships on a misty night.
A swirl of cigarette smoke
Traces ghost-like portraits in the air,
Highlighted by the ray of sun
That still lingers hazily there.

On the deep maroon aged carpet the emphasis falls,
Onto a small, now flood-lit cigarette-burned patch.
An almost near circle surrounding
charred black pillars of scorched weave,
Lay bare the crossover plastic threads,
far from its once illustrious past.
He doesn't care much for the sun putting
the spotlight on the decay of his home,
He won't watch any more.
He pulls the curtains to and lights another cigarette,
Stares the swirling ghosts of the past in the eye
And flicks the ash of his decline onto the floor.

The Children

Our little boy
Sat, leaning on the staircase.
Worry and confusion
Across his little face.
We were so caught up in our anger,
At first we didn't notice him there,
With the weight of the world on his shoulders,
Whilst his little sister slept upstairs.
It wasn't until we heard sobbing,
That we silenced the yells.
Hadn't noticed our frightened little son,
Too caught up in ourselves.
The children,
They have done nothing wrong.
Caught up in our futile war,
Where no child belongs.
We're supposed to protect them
Not put them in the firing line,
And it's no use blaming each other
For the fault was both yours and mine.
How do we explain to him,
That this is not his fault.
We selfishly thought it was just about us,
And this is the result.
We can't ever
Let this happen again
We need to put our differences aside,
We need to think about them.

The children,
They know so much more
Than we have ever
Given them credit for.
How could we neglect the greatest thing
That means the most to you and I.
Surely our differences – for a time –
Must be set aside.

The Road Between Us

There's a road between us,
That appeared so quick, brick by brick
And before we knew it – there it was.
We can see each other from either side,
But neither of us can cross.

There are no cars or lorries,
No bridges, no signs.
Just a tall, large clock on the very edge,
Loudly ticking out the passing time.

We both watch each other in silence,
We don't seem to know what to say.
All we know is that road between us
Is getting wider every day.

Who will make the first move
To try to get us reunited and back on track.
Before this road becomes totally impassable,
And then we'll have no choice but to step back.

I look at you, you seem to be a little bit hesitant,
Are we both unsure what we should do?
I thought you'd take that first step and run to me,
But it seems you expect me to come running to you.

We don't have that much time
And I'm not afraid to take that first step,
But I take one step BACK and then three more.
You look shocked, all the time expecting me to fall at your feet,
Which is the reason I built that road for.

Empty Boxes

Look around the room and all you'll see are empty boxes,
No treasured photographs of memories she can hold.
No journals and no diaries, no letters sent with love,
The boxes hold nothing of her life,
'cause there's no story to be told.
There's no treasured childhood teddy bear,
A forever friend in every way.
With scruffy fur and just one ear
That she would have loved until this day.
There's no graduation cap and gown,
No pictures with girlfriends acting the fool.
She didn't make friends easy,
And hardly went to school.
There's no handcrafted quilt from Grandma's,
For a young couple's first home together.
No picture of a loving man
She was going to love forever.
There's no wooden train from Grandpa
That he would have carved with love and joy.
A gift from the heart for his granddaughter's
First precious baby girl or boy.
There's no snapshots of holidays
With her children, laughing, by the sea.
No mementos of loved ones at Christmas time,
Because there is no family.
No Mother's Day card from a loving daughter
Thanking her for being her mum.
No outfit for her son's wedding day,
No grandchildren to dote on.
With no plans for the future,
And nothing of the past.
All she has is empty boxes,
And the dark shadows that they cast.

She could fill those boxes with broken dreams,
And they would overflow.
So maybe the boxes are best left empty,
Because regret is not a place she wants to go.
Her room is full of empty boxes,
Waiting for her story to begin,
But how long will she have to wait
Until she has something to put in.

The Last I Have of Him

As the storm clouds approached,
First came a gentle rain,
And I'm sure I saw you smiling
In the droplets on the windowpane.
But soon the shower became heavier,
And I no longer saw your face.
The rain had washed your memory away
And had left no trace.

I stood and watched the lightning,
And my hopes they soon soared
When I thought I saw you standing there
As the thunder roared.
For a moment the sky lit up
And illuminated all below,
I saw a figure by the tree,
And it was you, I know.

Mother Nature please let this storm
Last forever and ever.
It's the only time he and I
Can ever be together.
Send back the lightning,
The light rain and the wind.
So I can see him in the storm,
Because it's the last I have of him.

When the sun is shining,
He is not around.
Even in the shadows,
He cannot be found.
But in the brown autumn leaves
I feel his warmth,
And my hopes and wishes grow,
And as the cold winter comes around,
I see his footprints in the snow.

Mother Nature, unleash your power
Of a cold, wet or snowy day.
While others dread this weather,
It's for what I pray.
Just to see him for a second,
To me is everything,
And although he'll disappear –
When the storm clears,
I cherish the last I have of him.

A Few White Lies

I know you don't want me here,
I know you want me gone.
Just give me a couple of days,
And I'll be moving on.

I know we had a few cross words,
But they must have hurt you more than I thought,
And I know I told a few white lies,
But I guess I didn't think that I'd get caught.

My bags are waiting to be packed,
But it's all kind of sad.
I know we didn't always see eye to eye,
But it was a good thing that we had.

I may not have been totally honest,
You know talking is not really my thing,
But I have learned my lesson
By losing everything.

I hope you find someone better,
You surely deserve more.
I know I ruined my chances with you
By acting like a fool.

I can see it in your eyes,
How this has hurt you so bad.
So I'll be moving on,
Without the best thing I've ever had.

Her Place

She stands looking out of the large bedroom window,
A sad song playing in the background.
She's never felt so lost
And prays she'll soon be found.

Her heart is beating faster
Than she could possibly run,
But with just a single thought,
She knows this battle can't be won.

Her principal concern,
Her greatest fear
Is, there's nothing now
To keep her here.

Her eyes desperately search
For a point of light.
Her heavy heart struggles wearily,
Just to continue the fight.

Is this what she needs?
Is this a lesson to be learned?
Is her only hope of salvation
Yet to be earned?

On this thought she stands by the window again,
And waits patiently for night,
Hoping that the moon and stars
Will afford her some light.

She listens as she waits,
To the gathering winds.
The sound of the rushing through the bushes,
She tries to take in everything.

She then hears the small bird whistle,
Is he heralding in the eve?
The sky begins to darken,
Has the time come for her to believe?

She tries not to be disconcerted
With its slow transition
From the grey autumnal day – to night,
She feels she is drowning in her submission.

Surely she should not be tested,
As hard as she was being.
There was nobody there to help her,
No-one caring, no-one seeing.

She was being held captive,
All by herself.
She was doing this to her,
After all there was nobody else.

And when the stars
Finally showed their face,
She still felt lost
In her heart, her soul, her place.

The Guilt Clause (Claws)

I was afraid to hold him,
As his heartbeat for the last time,
And I prayed to God, the next to stop
Was going to be mine.

But mine kept going,
and I counted every laboured beat,
As the light left his eyes,
And he fell into a forever sleep.

There was nothing more painful that could break me,
There was no greater grief I could be in.
So why couldn't I hold him as we said goodbye,
Why did I break the promise I'd made to him?

To always protect him, to keep him safe,
To comfort him, no matter when or where,
But I let him down when he needed me most,
My arms not around him when he needed me there.

So much time has passed, five long years have gone,
But the heartache still burns cruelly on.
An ever-present guilt that haunts my every thought,
If only time could be bought.

I was just a few feet away from him,
As I held him tight before – and after he closed his eyes.
I was scared, so unprepared,
Didn't want to believe – this was the last time.

It's something you don't ever want to think about,
But at some point it comes looking for you,
But it's nothing like you expect it to be,
When that worst nightmare comes true.

It was because I loved him so much,
And not because I didn't love him
That I couldn't keep that promise,
Overwhelmed by the hell that I was in.

I know that he'd forgive me,
I know he'd understand.
I know he knew how much I loved him
But it doesn't change the fact –

That I can't forgive myself,
Although I comprehend the reason why.
I couldn't bear to hear his heart stop beating,
Because I knew it was goodbye.

I just couldn't do it,
Be it right – or be it wrong,
You don't want to hear silence,
Where once a precious heart beat strong.

Always my baby boy,
Always my best friend.
Always the guilt will haunt me,
For not holding him at the end.

Storm

The bird and beast
Sense something dark coming.
They fly, they hide,
And they start running.
Quickly the storm,
She takes the night.
The lightning's lustre,
Yellow, blue and white.
Across the sky,
Electric claws.
Thunder growls,
And then it roars.
The lightning fork
Sears the earth.
Cuts through the young tree,
Scorching the turf.
Grumbling, mumbling,
A dart – like rain sharply falls,
And Mother Earth cowers
As the thunder claps applause.
Soon followed by
The icy hail.
A twisted, angry,
Hard, white veil
That dents the soil
That it pounds
With striking, thrashing,
Thumping sounds.

And for an encore,
The storm is calling,
As the thunder echoes all around,
Like a thousand oak trees falling,
And the lightning coruscates, unrelenting,
Across the dark, mean skies.
Like a million lightbulbs, sporadically
Flashing before your eyes,
and for the grand finale,
A thunderbolt shakes the air,
One last note in her repertoire,
Then stillness everywhere.
The tumultuous clouds begin to clear,
Then falls a calm, soft rain,
Cool and gentle she caresses,
Easing the earth of all its pain.
Blue skies come
And push away
Any evidence
Of the grey,
But in another place, the bird and beast
Sense something dark is coming.
They fly away, and they hide,
They know it's time to start running.

Share My Last With You

We missed out on the best years of our lives,
But we can still share some together
But I'm worried it won't be enough,
Because I want to be with you forever.

And if you were to go first,
I wouldn't be far behind.
There would be nothing left for me here,
So I pray we have a lot of time.

A lot more time to share experiences
Neither of us might have done alone.
Time to explore each other's hearts and loves
That we've shielded wholly on our own.

A lot more time to make mistakes,
So we can put right the wrong.
A lot more time to share together,
So we are forever strong.

A lot more time to share our dreams,
So hand in hand we can see them through.
Let's make these the best years of our lives,
But I'm just satisfied I can share my last with you.

A More Beautiful Day to Say Goodbye

I don't want to sleep; I feel this is our last night together,
And although you've already gone, tomorrow I say goodbye.
I'm not sure if I want this aching night to end,
Because when it does, the closure means
You'll be no longer by my side.

The moon shines so bright in the perpetual darkness
And I wonder if it's as bright as the light you saw
When God decided it was time to call you home,
That beautiful, peaceful light that led you to his door.

The dawn is breaking,
I hear the small bird sing,
Outside I see the frost from the angels' frozen tears
Covering everything.

Outside the air is cold, but the sun is radiant,
There's not a single cloud in the sky.
God could not have gifted me
A more beautiful day to say goodbye.

Friends and family gather
To say farewell to you,
And amidst my desperate grief
I recall sweet memories too.

There's not a breath of wind in the air,
For a moment the earth is still,
And I silently tell you how much I love you
And how much I always will.

This ache that burns deep in my heart,
I know will pass as time goes by
And I'll always remember how God honoured your life
With such a beautiful day to say goodbye.

No Claws Required

The Coolest Cat in the Hood

He walks confidently
Down the street.
Like a bobby
Out on the beat.

He walks with his head
And his tail held high.
With an air of superiority
And a glint of mischief in his eye.

He leaps seamlessly
From fence to gate.
From way up high to way down low
He doesn't care to hesitate.

Not a slip, not a trip, a work of art in motion –
A gymnast would be inspired –
As he navigates every obstacle with just the brush of a paw,
So cool in fact, no claws required.

He knows that he's magnificent,
In the hood he's number one,
And the other cats, impressed by the poetry of it all,
Look longingly and wistfully on.

He arrives home and, still not finished with his repertoire,
Stands on his hind legs and taps on the door,
And just to make sure that he's been heard
He taps on it once more.

His smiling human opens the door,
He high-fives her and she strokes him,
And on noticing a wide-eyed awestruck passer-by
He bows to his adoring public before he slinks in.

Torn Between Missing Him and Loving You

Love doesn't always come straight away,
And sometimes it can take years for you to know,
At first you might even question
Whether you want this love to grow.
I loved him for a long, long time,
Right from the day we met,
And that love will last for eternity,
And I'm not sure I want to share it – yet.

I'm scared I'm going to let him down –
I don't want him to think that just because he's gone
That I've forgotten about him,
And I'm just moving on.
Even those words in themselves
Sound harsh and unforgiving,
Like I've packed his soul away,
Just so I can go on living.

But he'll be always and forever in my thoughts,
But now you are too,
And I'm torn between missing him –
And loving you.
You came into my life
When I needed a friend.
I didn't feel much for you at first –
I'm not going to pretend.

I always thought he'd be in my life,
But I guess that it just proves
No matter how strong your feelings are,
At any time, that precious love you could lose.
I know that he'd have liked you,
And he wouldn't want me to be on my own.
I know my heart is big enough for both of you,
Not just one special love alone.

You've been in my life now
For more than quite a while,
And I must admit I miss you when we're not together,
And I've come to love that sweet, sweet smile,
But it will always be a different love,
Still honest, real and true,
And it will bring me closer,
Where I'm still missing him – but loving you.

Beaten-Up Trucks and Sentimental Guys

He drives a beaten-up truck,
But only the best for it will do.
When it needed a panel changing, he refused a free offer,
Because it wasn't the 'exact' shade of blue.

His truck has seen some tough terrain,
And in parts, the rust holds her together.
She's certainly seen a few good miles
But he swears he'd never part with her ever.

He treats her like a lady,
She even has a name.
You have to take your shoes off before you get in,
So you don't damage the old girl's frame.

He won't tell anyone her name,
His friends already think he's crazy,
But the way he respects and loves that old truck
Never ceases to amaze me.

He bought her new alloy wheels when they lost their shine,
But only the very best ones you can get.
He says his lady deserves diamonds,
Like he'd ever let you forget.

When she sprang another oil leak,
He had tears in his eyes.
What is it with beaten up trucks and sentimental guys?

The Wordsmith

He could sell wings to angels,
Such was his way with words.
Make the mundane and the everyday
Sound like the most beautiful thing you've ever heard.

He could respectfully turn the most tragic of circumstances
Into a hope to commemorate.
Take the small successes in someone's life
And make them something big to celebrate.

In a few words he can tell the story
Of a family member that you never knew.
So honest and real, they become someone you feel
So much closer to.

The angels would gather to buy their wings –
Although they didn't really need them –
They just liked to sit and listen to the beautiful words
In the heavenly poetry he had written.

First Christmas Without You

I walked amongst the pine trees
Dusted with snow,
And the dancing light of the stars
Guided me where to go.

I came upon a glistening brook,
Its flowing water gentle and serene,
And I saw amidst the snow, white feathers,
Where the angels had been.

And there next to a wooden cross
A folded letter lay,
With words to bring comfort and peace
And take some of the pain away.

This is my first Christmas without you,
The first time we'll be apart,
But the angels have come to show me the way
To fix a broken heart.

The man walks amongst the pine trees,
Guided by the stars' light.
It's almost been a year now
Since he lost me, his loving wife.

He lays the roses by the wooden cross,
He sees the note and picks it up,
And he cries as he reads the tender words
That describe my enduring love.

It's his first Christmas without me
And he's been grieved and lost.
I watch beside the tree, my wings folded
As he places a kiss upon the cross.

I watch him for a minute
But I know I have to leave.
Mixed emotions about seeing him,
Because even angels grieve.

But at least he has some peace now
And he thanks the angels up above,
Especially the angel
Whom he had lost and loved.

I Wish

I wish I'd brought you flowers
Just that little bit more often,
And I wish I'd serenaded the butterflies
To dance around you in the garden.
I wish I'd painted rainbows
Onto every mean and darkened sky,
And regret haunts me,
Because I wish I had done all of this
Before we were compelled to say goodbye.

I wish every Christmas upon that beautiful tree,
I had placed on the top, a picture of you,
Because after all, you were the only
True angel that I knew.
And I wish I'd kept a snowflake,
One for every year we had together,
A unique beauty we could freeze in time
That would last – like our love – forever.

I wish I'd cherished more that burning flame,
Before it became a dying ember.
The flame in your heart that loved and protected me,
That precious light I'm scared I won't remember.
And I just wish you were still here
More than anything else at all,
Because the flowers, the butterflies
Mean nothing without you,
You're now the angel that I wish for.

Dirt Road Princess

She ran outside into the cool autumnal morning,
Smiled widely at her new shiny 'big girl' bike,
Pink and white ribbons tied on the handlebars
And the word 'princess' emblazoned on the saddle's side.
Over her ponytail she pulled the pink helmet on –
Her feet touching the pedals –
she slipped sideways on the leaves,
But she held on tightly, she could hear the trails calling
As determined she pushed forward, through gritted teeth.

You could hear her squeals of joy
Echo through the surrounding trees.
She was on a roll and her spirited soul
Had her riding that lively breeze.
Each new bumpy and muddy patch
She mastered with a thrill.
She felt so alive – holding tightly on
To the handlebars and her strong will.

Down the steep narrow ridge to the creek,
Her laughter jarring as she jolted up and down.
There was no one around to hear her – but
She kind of liked the sound.
Then she speeded up and took the trail by the tail
Behind, her tyre marks left the art she had etched,
Then an indescribable feeling danced in her tummy
As her feet left the pedals, her legs outstretched.

She felt like she was flying,
The feeling buzzed throughout her soul
As she flew down the dirt road –
no restraints – and in control.
She put her feet firmly back on the pedals again –
Time had passed so quickly – she had to head back,
So with a confident skid she turned around
And headed excitedly home up that track.

The ride back, although exhilarating
Also made her feel kind of sad.
The dirt road is her castle in the sky
And it's the best fun she's ever had.
When she arrives home, that bike no longer shines,
Both she and the bicycle from top to toe are a muddy mess,
But tomorrow she'll wash the bike and make it shine again,
Ready for another adventure – this little dirt road princess.

His Baby

When his baby was born,
She was born asleep
But he wanted to see her
So her memory he could keep.

And though he gently held her,
He knew that she was gone,
But in that precious moment, he also knew
His little girl had been someone.

But then there was denial,
And his wife and he couldn't talk.
They had so much to say to each other
But feared what would happen if they opened up.

Their confusion and anger,
Why had this happened to them?
They were good, strong people,
And they questioned the Lord again.

They struggled with what had happened,
And they doubted their belief.
If there was a god, how could he let this happen?
Their souls were lost in pain and grief.

But slowly, they began to talk candidly with the Lord,
And their faith started to recover.
They felt his strength, his love, his hope,
And they began talking to each other.

They talked about their hopes and dreams,
Of what they had wanted for their little girl,
And many nights their tears would come,
She was a real gift to this world.

There would never be full closure,
But as the months came and passed,
They remembered the short time they shared with her,
And how that precious memory would always last.

They'd never forget their daughter,
They had their memory to keep
Of holding her, knowing she was their little girl,
Although she was born asleep.

The Kids

Young Love – Tale With a Twist

They sat in the diner, a few nervous words
Over strawberry milkshakes and Mississippi mud pie.
Each shyly taking a glance at each other,
Soon laughing together as tongues got tied.
When their laughter calmed,
So did their first-date nerves,
And she blushed a little
As he pulled his chair up next to hers.
And when the jukebox began playing,
He held out his hand and gently pulled her up,
They danced through songs – both fast and slow,
Until the music stopped.
They sat down, exhausted,
Both could not stop smiling,
They eagerly ate mouthfuls of dessert,
Appetites and comfortable excitement rising.
Then her mobile rang and she took it from her purse,
Suddenly despondent she answered the phone.
Sadly, she already knew who it was,
Telling her it was late and it was time to come home,
She tried to get an extra hour,
But there was no convincing them.
She put her phone away and dolefully looked at him
And said 'He's picking us up at ten.'
She looked so downcast
And he felt it too,
But her smile quickly returned
When he said 'Let's do this again – soon.'
They both giggled as she slipped her hand in his
As they headed to the door to meet their ride.

He quickly ran a comb through his hair,
Knowing he had to make a good impression
to the man waiting outside.
Into the cool air he saw the man standing by the car door.
As he walked over to him and said 'Hello, son,'
There were smiles all round as they got into the car,
And the driver turned and whispered 'I'm happy for you,
MUM.'
You see, these two new sweethearts
Were both in their seventies,
Who says that young love
Should be just for the kids.

The Anger (The Perfect Storm)

The vultures that circle overhead
Nobody else is seeing.
The physical pain of a gathering storm of emotion
Attacks every fibre of my being.
The anger forms like a whisper of cloud
That becomes a hurricane,
Ready to devastate what's left of my spirit
In a fury of wind barbed with pain.

I'm defenceless to stop it,
Although the warning has been audible for some time.
It's an anger set to bring chaos
Into an already lawless mind.
This is all directed to destroy my soul,
But it's more than an anxious rancour,
This is hurt, loss and fear bonding together
That has borne this spiteful anger.

I feel like I'm going crazy,
For all I know, I'm already there,
But this feels so much more than madness,
I'm sure 'crazy' would be easier to bear.
Every harsh emotion I have struggled with
Has taken on an infrangible form,
And when anger connected it
became the final link in the chain
And so was created the perfect – self-destructive – storm.

Gordon – The Smartest Giraffe – Ever!

Gordon is bright and very clever,
He is the smartest giraffe – EVER!

Gordon wears cool purple glasses
And reads aloud in English classes.

He can speak Japanese, German and French,
Crocodile, tiger and elephant.

He's a well-known writer of 'jungle books'
And he's won awards for his good looks.

His number-one hit was top of the pops
And he's modelled for *Vogue* in pink flip flops.

He's won an Oscar for a starring role
And scored a winning cup match goal.

He's bungee jumped from a balloon
And captained a space shuttle to the moon.

But the best thing ever, Gordon will say,
Is learning new things every day.

Yes, Gordon is bright and very clever,
He is the smartest giraffe – EVER!

A Church Without Bells

I walk across the dirt road
To where the trees had once been.
For years a beautiful forest,
In every shade of brown and green.
I used to come here as a girl,
Play in the leaves and wood,
So I came to see this place one more time
Before they put that factory up.

But it's like a church without bells,
Cold and quiet – nothing left of the place that I remember.
Like a fire without heat,
Growing colder with that last burning ember.
The heart has stopped beating,
Its soul has gone,
And the sky is grey in mourning
Where the warm sun once shone.

And it breaks my heart to see
Nothing left of where it used to stand,
Now, like a church without bells,
It's a sad and silent land.
For a while I kick the dirt around,
Hoping that I'll find
A little bit of something
Maybe left behind.

But all there is – is just broken earth,
A few splinters of wood,
And I walk away, tears rolling down my face,
Knowing that it's really gone for good.
Like a church without bells,
Like a memory long lost.
Like a bridge to salvation
That cannot be crossed.

Like a wish that's been granted
But has never come true.
Like the will of a million,
overturned by the few.
Someone who has all the answers
But keeps quiet and never tells.
This place now bears a silence, where joy once rang out,
Like a church without bells.

The Sweetest Kiss

He pulled me gently towards him,
And as our lips met,
He kissed me so purely, so tenderly,
It's a kiss I will never forget.
And as he held me safely in his arms,
I prayed this would be my life forever more,
Because he touched in me something so absolute,
A sweet honesty I'd never felt before.

That loving kiss lingered on my lips,
For many nights and many days,
And I know that I'll remember it
Forever and always.
But that beautiful, wonderful moment
Is not exactly as it seems,
Because that kind, gentle man with the sweetest kiss
Was only in my dreams.

In the Air

The little girl would fly back and forth
Joyfully on her swing.
Then after a little while,
She'd begin to sing.
A gentle voice, pure and sweet,
Even the birds would stop to listen.
Her young voice as honey-gold as her long hair
That in the sunshine glistened.
And she would sing all the songs
Her dad played on the radio,
Making up her own innocent words
To the parts of the songs she didn't know.
The neighbours would go out to their gates to watch her –
And she'd sing crystal clear and loud as she soared –
All except the man who lived beyond the far end of her garden
Who would walk down to his house and
dramatically slam the door.
She would go on singing,
Until her mom called her in for tea.
After her meal, she'd finish all her chores,
Then she'd go back on the swing, singing happily.
She'd be there, whatever the weather,
She'd wear red wellies, a yellow plastic hat in the rain,
A long, flowered dress and tennis shoes in the sun
And a big, warm hat and coat when the winter came.
It's been four decades since then, she's grown up and moved away,
Her old house now run down and boarded up,
But that rusted old swing still stands in the high grass,
A lasting symbol of innocence and childhood love.
The neighbours – still around – remember her.
Sometimes they think that she's still there,
Because when they stop and listen, with the birds,
Her voice is still carried in the air.

Days of Our Lives

The huge cobweb looked like a tennis net,
Stretching right across Mom's washing line.
Even across the wooden prop
That held up the wire from time to time.

It looked absolutely beautiful
In the morning dew.
Glistening pear drops, like diamonds
And so cleverly intricate too.

I didn't care for the spider,
Curled up right on the edge of the web.
It was either very big,
Or extremely well fed.

My eyes had watched – too long – the beast,
As if I weren't scared enough,
But I still had a lot of chores to do,
And number one was pegging the washing up.

Mom had said it might not dry,
But hopefully it will blow,
And had shouted after me,
Wipe the line along as you go.

Then my younger brother came outside,
Bravely said 'I'll get that spider down,
You can't put the washing up
With that creepy thing around.'

I'm sure I saw a little bead of sweat
Form upon his brow.
Was he a little nervous too?
But he was all I had right now.

He slowly walked over to the beastie
And gently picked her up,
Put her on a flowerbed,
Was this really my little bruv?

My brother lifted his arms and said
'I have nerves of steel,
Sis, that spider won't be back,
It really wasn't a big deal.'

I felt a strange feeling come over me,
I stood up to kiss him but saw his shaking knees.
I think he knew what I had planned to do,
And he wouldn't have been too pleased.

I ran inside to get the washing
And a cloth to remove the dew.
The weight lifted off my shoulders
And finally I knew.

My little brother was not so little any more,
He'd grown in front of my eyes.
Today I'd experienced every emotion
From fear and anxiety to pride and surprise.

And then, when he offered to help
Put the washing up,
In that moment, instead of amazement
I just felt overwhelmed with love.

It had taken this 'something'
To make me realise
That baby I had once changed
Was now a thoughtful young man,
And it was one of the best days of our lives.

Once You Leave

Once you leave
I know you're never coming back,
And it just breaks my heart to know
One day it will come to that.

And I'm torn because I don't know
What I'm supposed to do,
Because it kills me to think of you being gone
Every time I look at you.

I'll do everything I can to keep you here,
But the time is coming soon, I know
That God is going to tell his angels to come,
That it's time for you to go.

A life without you
I just cannot conceive,
And I'm not sure how I'll go on
Once you leave.

I just want to hold you
And never let you go,
But I've become afraid to get too close
Because I'm losing you, I know.

It's not that I don't love you,
It's that I love you too much,
And I don't want to think that the next time I hold you,
It might be our very last touch.

I'm trying to prepare myself
For what's about to be.
I don't want to think about tomorrow,
It might be the day that you leave me.

But I don't want to spend the time we have
Preparing to grieve.
I need to save those countless tears
For once you leave.

So I'm going to try and make this the best time,
In God's wisdom I believe,
And I pray we have just a little more time
Before you finally leave.

Before She Got Old

It's a curious place,
Some might say,
A hoarder's paradise
In each and every way.

But I wonder what secrets
Those overflowing boxes hold
From her past life,
Before she got old.

It's a curious place,
not at all what it seems,
Behind all the rubbish
Hide secrets and lost dreams.

She can't remember
What's crammed on each self.
All she keeps saying is
'I'm so ashamed of myself.'

She tells me when she was younger
She kept things in good order.
Now what's there, she can't even guess.
Then I jump as she cries out loud 'It's all such a mess!'

Her tears fall freely
Of how life beat her down.
Now not even her treasures
Will ever be found.

I offer to assist her,
I'm just trying to help,
But she says it's all her mess,
And she will do it herself

But both of us know
This disease is unstoppable,
And to do this all herself
Would be nothing short of impossible.

Then she gets quite angry,
Warns me not to mess with her things,
But I understand it's all she has,
It's her everything.

Her life in papers,
Photographs of good times,
People she's lost,
Friends she's left behind.

Like a brittle branch of an autumnal tree,
She can barely lift a cup.
It would take her another lifetime
To sort out and tidy up.

We talk for a while.
She tells me how things got so bad,
And she's not sure she wants to remember
All the years she's had.

She's so frightened that I'll judge her,
Maybe rest my eyes too long on a photograph.
I'll ask too many questions
About how she got on the wrong path.

It's a curious place,
In need of a tidy and a dust,
But until – if she ever agrees –
I shouldn't ask too much.

Then she surprises me when she says
'I think it's old bills and stuff like that,
So I'd appreciate the help,
If you've not taken the offer back.'

And for the first time I see a look of mischief twinkle in her eye,
And I know I've gained her trust
When she smiles and says 'You do the heavy work, dear
And I will casually dust!'

We both worked hard
And made some space.
How different she looked
With an unworried smile on her face.

Her cheeks held a gentle pink blush
That made her look twenty years younger,
And when I momentarily stopped for a gulp of juice
She cheekily said 'Come on, hurry dear,
we don't have much longer.'

Now it's not the room
That's curious to see.
It's she who has sparked
My curiosity.

I find things representing her past life,
An illustrious singing career,
Her stint on Broadway,
Amazing stories you'd never guess were hidden here.

Why isn't she basking
In the memories of her success?
But when I ask, she whispers
'Yesterday's gone' under her breath.

Then a sadness clouds her eyes,
She talks of how she used to be so bold,
So confident, a somebody –
Before she got old.

The Crow

Atop the highest branch
Out in the rain
Sits the dark black silken crow
Surveying his kingdom once again.
Whatever the weather
He's there everyday,
And not a little drop of rain
Will keep him away.
But I can't figure out
What else there is above
That keeps that slight, little branch so strong,
That small branch that holds him so proudly up.
Maybe he's made of dark coal dust,
Or the branch made of iron ore,
Is it just a trick of the light,
And he's not real at all?
He isn't looking my way,
But I know he's watching me,
And I wonder what it is he hides
That I cannot see.
Then in a second he sweeps down,
Close enough for me to touch, to feel,
And I wonder if he's just establishing his validity,
Proving he's not an illusion, he's all real.
Then he's back up atop the highest branch,
Way up in that tree
And he knows I'm none the wiser
As I stand watching him, watching me.

Money Counts for Nothing

It isn't easy
When you have to explain –
To the kids – they can't have expensive things
Time and time again.
You put in every hour
Just to get the bills paid
And have little to show material-wise
For the sacrifices that you've made.

But the kids always have clean clothes,
Their tummies are always fed,
And Daddy does amazing voices
When he reads stories to them in bed.
They may not have a lot
Of what this new world brings
But you can't outbid love
With material things.

A fancy cell phone may be good
Until it gets out of date,
And a telephone cannot fix
A heart when it breaks.
Designer clothes may look great
And give you a certain style,
But nothing looks better
Than a warm and loving smile.

Love is priceless,
It's something that you cannot buy,
And you can't put a price on being
The apple of someone's eye.
Money counts for nothing
If your heart's not satisfied,
And love is a treasure for everyone,
It's just a treasure that you can't buy.

The Hardest Goodbye

Sometimes the hardest goodbyes
Are the ones that we are all there for,
And you don't want to let her go,
Because you couldn't love her more.

It seems so unfair, it came so quick,
You probably wish that you had known,
But God knew she was tired and weary,
And he whispered for her to come home.

She had bounded into your lives
And your jigsaw was complete.
She snuggled up inside your hearts
And became the strong heartbeat.

Now the loss is so difficult,
And you can't bear to think that she's gone,
But you only have to touch your chest
And in your heartbeat feel her spirit living on.

I know you wish you'd had a little more time,
But no amount would have been enough,
You wanted to make sure she knew how much she meant to you,
But I guarantee she knew she was loved.

Sometimes the hardest goodbyes
Are the ones that we are all there for,
And like how you watched over her,
She now watches over you,
Because she couldn't love you more.

Where the Truth Lies

You could always influence the judge
And manipulate the facts.
You'd cry when you spoke of your poor childhood
From the wrong side of the tracks.
This time you 'sincerely' told how you regretted
Everything in the past you had done.
You swore this time you were telling the truth
And you weren't prepared for what was to come.

The judge said the 'proof' outweighed your story,
But she complimented you on your acting ability,
And she sentenced you as the gavel came down,
Then they carted you off to the county facility.
Before, you'd always got away
From justice and the law,
So how does it feel now,
Behind that prison door?

I was once a pawn in your game,
And now – for what it's worth,
Congratulations – you once played me for a fool,
But in the end I got justice served.
You see, the judge had all the evidence,
You'd done the crime – there was decisive proof,
Except I kind of manipulated it,
And for once you'd been telling the truth.

This time you were not the perpetrator,
But I convinced them all,
Managed to fool a good, smart judge
To contribute to your downfall.
You see, after you wronged me,
I just couldn't rest.
So I hatched a plan to give justice a nudge –
Well, I did learn from the best!

You've only got three years to serve,
I hope you change your ways,
Though I must admit, it was kind of true when you said
'Who says crime doesn't pay?'
If you're on your best behaviour, you'll be out in two,
And if you'd like to know – for what it's worth –
You were right when you said crime sometimes pays,
Because my crime got you what you deserved.

Hand in Hand

The older couple on the bench
Sitting next to me
Were talking about their next holiday
So excitedly.

Then I heard the man say something
That made my heart beat loud and fast.
He said 'You know that this holiday
Will probably be our last.'

They talked so happily
Of going back to where they first met,
And she said 'Let us make more memories
Before we have chance to forget.'

There was no sadness in their voices,
They didn't dwell on the times that had gone,
And it made me realise how precious time is
With your special one.

Then they got up and walked away,
Still discussing their plans
Like two young lovers first time in love
They walked affectionately hand in hand.

You Were My Voice, Dad
(Now it's My Time to Be Yours)

I was just a child,
My small voice couldn't be heard above the crowd.
That's when you would step in, Dad,
Your voice was strong and loud.

Everybody listened,
They really didn't have a choice,
You were firm but gentle,
A strong command to your voice.

But time has changed everything,
Your voice now quiet and weak.
It's my time to be your voice now,
For you I need to speak.

How I wish things
Were the way they used to be,
But age has turned the tables,
The baton handed to me.

There is something written
In the 'daughter clause',
You used to be my voice, Dad,
Now it's my time to be yours.

You'll always be my hero, Dad,
In my eyes always strong and proud,
And I promise I will do for you
The very best I can.

You were clear and put your case,
Said what needed to be said.
Now I'm the one who needs to speak up
And make them listen to me instead.

You were the lion
Whose roar could not be ignored.
You were my voice, Dad
Now it's time for this lioness to be yours.

The Price You Pay for Loving

When you left, my heart stopped for a second,
And ever since then
It has never beat in the same way,
It's never been the same again.
It once beat for a purpose,
And that purpose was you.
But in a heartbeat you were gone and I was broken,
And my grieving heart took it badly too.
The price you pay for loving
Comes at a huge cost,
And no matter how much money you have
It can't come close to what you've lost.
That love was so priceless,
Now I feel I've been left with nothing,
I may still have all the sweet memories,
But pain's the price you pay for loving.
When I think to when we met,
Never thought about time running out.
Thought we'd both live forever,
I had no fears, I had no doubts.
Your love gave me confidence,
There was nothing I couldn't face,
Never crossed my mind I'd ever be in
Such a heart-breaking, lonely place.
I just expected it to go on always,
In forever I believed,
Was I so happy in the present, I ignored the future,
Or was it that I was just too naive?
Everything has changed for me,
And no material things can stop the suffering,
But I guess the hurt and tears that come after loss
Are the price you pay for loving.

Because There Just Ain't

Dedicated to the 'real nan', Dorothy Watts xxx

She reminded me of Grandma,
Same curly hair and flowered skirt.
Because she looked so much like her.
She had that air about her,
Her sweetness and her light,
But she didn't have that telling little sparkle
That made Grandma's eyes so bright.

But that's hardly surprising,
Grandma was one of a kind,
Beautiful in heart and soul,
A sharp wit and a sharp mind,
With the wisdom of a tribal chief
And the patience of a saint,
You'll never find anyone like her
Because there just ain't.

Tiny, but she could hold her own,
Give me advice that only Grandma could.
No subject ever out of bounds,
Taught me to be careful if I couldn't be good.
She had a lot of mischief,
So smart, so sweet, so funny,
Enticed the most desirable of men,
Giving younger women a run for their money.

She was one of a kind,
She was stand alone,
Breathtakingly unparalleled,
Like no one I've ever known,
With the wisdom of a tribal chief,
And the patience of a saint,
I never found another like her,
And it's because there just ain't.

Now she's up in heaven,
Teaching patience to the saints,
And there's not another angel like her,
Because there just ain't.

He Never Came Home

I know he's cradled in your arms,
I know he's safe with you there,
But it doesn't make the grief in my heart
Any easier to bear.
I know that in time
It will all make sense to me,
But at this moment in my life, Lord,
All that I can see
Is that he never came back,
He never came home.
We went there together
Then I came back alone.
I've never felt such pain,
I'm broken, I'm angry,
I'm questioning my faith in you,
And why you took him from me.
I can't see how it will get easier
When you left me behind,
But people tell me to have faith in you,
And there will come a time
When one day I'll appreciate your wisdom,
When I'll realise he needed your care,
and I'll finally understand he never came home
Because with you, Lord – he was already there.

I Don't Have a Plan

I don't have a plan,
Ideas not many – but fewer
And where I am going,
I'm not really sure.

All I can do
Is the best that I can,
Well, what else can you do
When you don't have a plan?

Not sure of the road you are travelling,
Not sure what to expect.
When you don't have a plan,
You have no idea what to do next.

I'll give my everything,
I'll make a stand,
But where will it get me
When I don't have a plan?

I'll just keep on trying
To find the right path,
Concentrating on forward
And not looking back.

There's none so wise
As those who can
Navigate their lives
By having a plan.

I'd love to have a plan,
But at the end of the day
It's not who I am,
Because life always gets in the way.

The Black-and-White Picture

It's so obvious to see
You've fallen in love again.
Like when we first met,
Just not the same.
You can't hide your love for her,
Not one single bit,
And I'm not the only one
To mention it.

She's been on your mind
For such a long time – and yet
You've never, ever kissed her,
You haven't even met.

All you've had is a black-and-white picture
For all this time,
And you're so in love with just the thought of her
You've put her picture in your wallet, next to mine.

You've been buying her little gifts
And I've pretended not to see,
You had thought it was exciting
Hiding it from me.

And no matter what we were doing,
No matter where we were,
You always set aside some time each day
So you could talk to her.

You've never been embarrassed,
You didn't care who heard,
And it was obvious when you said you loved her
That you meant every word.

Now eight months on
Into your love affair,
You were finally going to meet her,
And there was no doubt I'd be there.

Just before she arrived,
I admitted to you my fears,
And I can't deny that I was in pain
And we both shared our tears.

But to see you smile when you met her,
I would not have swapped for the whole world.
Your love affair was finally reality
As you cradled her, our new baby girl.

It's Time to Be a Man

You're old enough and now scared enough
To know what you have done.
You could be a father
Through one reckless night of fun.

You never thought it could happen to you,
You always dodged the bullet somehow.
Now you can't be a coward and hide yourself away,
It's what you do that matters now.

It's time to take responsibility
And plan for the hard work that's to come.
Are you prepared to stick around
Or are you going to run?

It's time to face the consequences
And do everything you can
To show you can step up to the plate,
It's time to be a man.

You've always been used to fleeing
When things haven't gone your way.
Are you now mature enough
To know this time you need to stay?

You're going to have to work hard now,
But your reward will bring so much joy,
Being a father changes your life
And makes a man out of a boy.

I know it's not just you to blame,
But prove to everyone you have what it takes
To work on nurturing a future that is good
And acknowledging your mistakes.

You're going to prove the doubters wrong
And do everything you can,
Because you know the time is now,
And it's time to be a man.

With love and hard work, your child will grow strong,
And he'll appreciate what he has,
And you'll know you've become a real man
When he wants to be just like his dad.

Forgotten

She sits in the old chair,
A thin blanket on her knee.
She cannot afford to pay
For both food and heat.
Her legs ache so badly
From the rheumatism,
But nobody seems bothered,
No one wants to listen.
The arthritis bites
Into every bone,
But she hardly gets visits
So tries to brave it on her own.
She sits in that old chair,
In pain and poverty,
The only way to keep warm
A thin blanket on her knee.

She worked hard all her life,
Rarely took a day off sick,
And now she sadly wonders
How it has come to this.
She was one of many who made this country great,
The sacrifice alone was hers.
So a little help and respect right now
Is the least that she deserves.
But she's quit asking,
Promises were made – but she's still waiting,
She doesn't like to be a bother,
She knows services are at the point of breaking.

So she sits in her old chair
So much time – she thinks a lot –
But she can't help feeling hopeless
As she feels every second of the ticking clock.
She sits there every day,
A thin blanket on her knee.
One of millions – forgotten –
And the hidden shame of this country.

One Step Too Far

The last coal mine is closing,
It's the end of an era.
This 'new world' they talk about
Seems to get one step nearer.
But could losing the familiar
End up leaving us feeling empty?
Challenge our dignity
And make us lose our identity.

The industrial revolution
Made us what we are.
So is losing it, bit by bit,
Just one step too far?
The world is constantly changing,
And life keeps moving on,
But there will be no going back
When these things have all gone.

The television news only seems to be
Wall-to-wall tragedy, famine and war,
But we all now seem to be immune to it,
Because we've seen it all before.
Our weather patterns are changing,
It's something we should not ignore.
So why is it we seem to be doing less,
When we should be doing more?

There are cities underwater,
Rivers breached, deluged with rain,
And all we do is make excuses
And say 'This can't happen again.'
Then when the flood is gone, streets dry again,
We seem to forget how things were and move on.
Will we regret not acting on the warning signs
When our chances are all gone?

Are we too complacent?
Are things happening too fast?
Are we really learning the lessons
From mistakes we've made in the past?
Some things are inevitable,
But has our wisdom been dumbed down?
Are we just accepting worrying changes
Where resolutions could be found?

Still families are just existing in poverty,
Whilst for others the champagne never runs out.
This country is quickly losing direction,
Whilst the politicians just sneer and shout.
And that last coal mine is closed now,
Communities lie fractured forever.
This country has never been so broken,
Drifting apart when we need to pull together.

We can't make excuses any more,
We need to build, we need to dream, we need to mend.
Let it be the start of a new hope-filled beginning
And not the beginning of a sad, regretful end.

Going home

He ran the pavements,
He ran the grass.
He didn't think that
He could run so fast.

Into the woods,
He nervously swam across the lake,
In between nettles and stones,
Trying to think of the fastest route he could take.

Was he running from?
Or was he running to?
People he passed were sure they recognised him,
He was a boy they felt they knew.

And they watched as he jumped fences,
Ran through streets and across rails.
He had no time to speak when someone asked
If 'the devil was on his tail'.

He knew the clock was ticking,
He had no time to waste.
This was one appointment
For which he could not be late.

With seconds to spare he reached the cabin door
And went inside to where his ailing grandma lay.
He knelt down and held her hand gently
As she smiled at him, then peacefully passed away.

He had promised her every day
That he would not be late,
Now he stood up and unfurled his pure white wings
To lead his grandma home to Heaven's gate.

It had been exactly one year
Since he had fallen into the lake and drowned,
And every night since he'd come to speak to grandma
He knew the reason he was still around.

They had talked and laughed and cried,
And even though she knew he was gone,
She was sure he'd keep his promise
To take her home when her time had come.

Together they took that final journey
He had once travelled on his own.
Grandmother and grandson – hand in hand –
Were finally going home.

In Those Four Walls

In the same room he sits, both day and night,
Cobwebs covered in dust,
And on the old plastic table, a chipped metal plate
So old and worn it's starting to rust.
The outsides of the windows are covered in dirt
From the countless storms and passing rain.
The grit and the damp are now coming through
From a crack in the windowpane.

The newspaper he is reading
Is over three weeks old,
And he wears the same woollen tweed coat
Because his big house gets so cold.
His old, battered tobacco tin
Has long since lost its gloss,
Constantly reaching for this constant companion,
The tin's lettering has rubbed off.

Brown paper bags stained with vinegar and salt
Are strewn across the tiled floor,
And polystyrene trays are carefully stacked
Against the bare, hard wall.
This is not a man aged with time-worn bones,
He's a young man – well in his prime,
But he's cut himself off from most of the outside world,
And in those four walls now spends most of his time.

He likes the familiar of his unkempt room.
Any pride he once had has long since faded.
He knows his skin looks sallow and old,
His weary face lined and jaded.
But he's relieved he has nothing left to lose,
His own built reality in just those four walls,
He feels lucky to have escaped from a cruel, mean world,
And he's glad that he has no friends who call.

He lights up another cigarette,
He doesn't care to think of days of old.
He sits back in the hard wooden chair
And pulls his jacket around him to keep out the biting cold.
He doesn't much change his routine, he likes it as it is,
He likes the order and control that is his alone.
For him it gives sense and a meaning to his life,
The solitude for him, the only real thing he owns.

A long time gone

My eyes momentarily fell onto the old lady
Until she glanced my way.
It was clear we both felt uncomfortable,
So I didn't look her way again.

I desperately wanted to observe her,
Just so I could be sure,
But I felt uneasy,
So I didn't look any more.

If it was her, she would have recognised me,
I can be sure of that,
But as I walked away
I couldn't help but look back.

Just in case in her glance
She didn't clearly see,
So as I walked away, I walked slowly,
So she could get a better look at me.

I strained my ears to listen,
Just in case she called my name.
Disappointed, I heard nothing,
So I strained to listen again.

Maybe she hadn't seen me staring,
Maybe our eyes had made no connection,
Although the unease had seemed mutually palpable,
Perhaps she had just glanced in my direction.

As I walk away,
We're out of each other's view,
And I begin to worry,
What if it was her I knew?

But deep inside my heart,
I know that it couldn't be,
Because that beautiful woman
A long time ago left me.

But that old lady walked through my thoughts
From the day into the night.
I was sad and lost in the hope
I could just have been right.

I prayed all through the night,
She could be the one
I cripplingly lost
A long time gone.

You Can't be the Remedy
(When You are the Cause)

You can't be the remedy
When you are the cause.
You can't be the cavalry
When you started the war.
You can't be the white flag
When you're still aiming your gun.
You can't be the ending
When you've only just begun.

You can't be the church
If you side with the devil.
You can't be at the top of the hill
If the playing field is level.
You can't be perfection
When you have so many flaws.
You can't be the remedy
When you are the cause.

You can't be the wrong
That thinks it's always right.
You can't be the sun
In the middle of my night.
You can't be the mirror
When you give back no reflection.
You can't be the compass
When you have no sense of direction.

You can't be the sheriff
When you make up your own laws.
You can't be the remedy
When you are the cause.

If You Love Her Still

You know how much I love you,
And you say you love me too,
But I have an uneasy feeling,
And I don't mean to doubt you,
But I can't measure up to her,
And I never will.

For both of us, we have to end it now,
If you love her still.
I don't want to lose you
But understand, I can't risk taking
The chance of falling deeper for you
When my heart's already breaking.

So if you love her still,
It's better that you go.
Would you be thinking of her when you kissed me?
I would never know.
I want to be with you forever,
But I can't – until
You've got it clear in your mind
If you love her still.

I know how much she meant to you,
She's sure to be on your mind,
But it can't work with you and me
Unless you leave her behind.
I'm not angry with you,
You can't simply forget someone at will,
But you need to be honest with her and me,
If you love her still.

If you love her still,
Then you must let her know.
I can't bear this uncertainty,
And if it's her – I'll have to go.
I don't feel bad about her,
If you two are meant to be.
I'll walk quietly out your life,
You'll get no anger from me.

But I can't do this forever,
So please – promise me you will
Tell me if we stand a chance,
Or if you love her still.
I think you know that you have to leave,
And although I fear that you will,
I know I have to let you go,
Because I love YOU still.

And He'd Run

He hadn't paid his bills,
Then one night the lights went out,
But he had his trusty torch
So he could get about.
And when the sheriff came calling,
He did what he'd always done.
He took off out the back door
And he'd run.

He was never short of girlfriends,
Whom he had lots of fun with,
He may have been a coward,
But he had a lot of love to give.
But when his latest girl suggested
That she should move in,
He put on those sneakers –
Commitment just wasn't for him.

To keep afloat, to get by,
Gambling was his game,
And he would pay for everyone
When the beer came.
But one night he got in over his head,
And for the first time in years, he hadn't won,
So he politely headed for the bathroom,
Opened the window and he'd run.

He always seemed to bounce back,
It seems being a coward worked for him.
He figured if it got too rough,
To run would be win-win.
But when he stopped with friends one autumn night,
The campfire's sparks seemed awfully high,
Then he watched as one caught on the cabin roof,
Where his friend lay asleep inside.

Whilst other friends stood in shock,
He did what he had always done.
He tied his laces tight,
And he began to run.
But this time the story's different,
He didn't run away.
He ran and pulled his friend from the fire
And got him out of harm's way.

Whilst some doused the fire,
Others gathered around him.
They patted his back, and all agreed
It was the most heroic thing they had ever seen.
So I guess maybe a coward
Is not the worst thing to be after all,
Because he became a hero
When people needed one most of all.

The First Year Without Santa Claus

Another family broken
For another heart-breaking reason.
One of many across the land
Who now dread their once favourite season.
The first year the little girl won't get her traditional stocking.
The first time in six decades the older man will be alone.
No gingerbread house or Christmas tree
That was once part of their festive Christmas home.

The Christmas cards pile through her door,
And she cries a tear for every one.
She puts them away in the bottom of a drawer,
It's just not Christmas without her mom.
The first year without that special pudding
That she loved to make.
The first year we just couldn't have
The family photograph without her,
That Grandpa so loved to take.

The little boy who wrote to Santa
With only one thing written on his list,
But Santa shakes his head with sadness because he knows
He can't grant that little boy's wish.
The first year without that safe, comforting hug
She would drive four hundred miles for,
And she wonders how can Christmas ever be
A celebration any more.

The first time the close-knit family
Will not be all together,
Bringing the sad realisation
That even the strongest love can't last forever.
The first year without that Christmas Day walk,
The pounding of excited paws,
Where grief is cast over many different lives,
Their first year without Santa Claus.

Tracking Erika

They are watching her every move
As she storms across the sea,
Plotting co-ordinates and running through numbers,
Trying to figure out how bad she could be.
But she's more than just colour on a satellite,
Hurricane Erika, as she is known,
She is Mother Nature's wild daughter
And has destructive plans of her own.

A calm, dark, velvet sky
Reveals a crescent moon,
But Hurricane Erika is on her way
And will make landfall soon.
And she will dance
Across plain and field,
The earth will bow in reverence
And its land will yield.

She will whip and whirl
The trees and the dust
And level houses
In just one gust.
People hurrying, working hard
To make sure the warning goes out,
So that windows are boarded and streets deserted
When Erika unveils her clout.

There will be no welcoming party for her,
But she doesn't need a crowd.
There will be no doubt of her presence,
She is violent, angry and loud.
And soon the air is flushed with leaves,
Wooden fences and broken trees,
All gathered up, then scattered around
Onto a devastated, torn up ground.

The ranches' horses buck and neigh
As they're quickly and safely led away,
Whilst cars and vans are tossed and turned
And electricity cables fizz and burn.
In the dark, tumultuous sky
The thunder and lightning come,
A fanfare to see out Erika,
Who is almost done.

Soon Erika is gone,
And there's a gentle whisper of wind
That is hardly noticed and then is gone,
But behind the scenes, people are running through numbers,
Erika maybe finished, but there is more to come.

Without Intention

You weren't trying to hurt me,
And I know you didn't mean to be unkind,
But the innocent words got twisted
In my fearful and fragile mind.
It has caused me so much sorrow,
And too much pain to mention,
But I don't put any blame on you,
Because it was said without intention.

It's something you'll learn about me,
That sometimes the innocuous words you say
Kind of get distorted
And touch me in a different way.
You have to see that I don't think
In the same way that you do.
Words can seem more hurtful
Than they would seem to you.

I know we have something special,
And you've brightened up my life,
But a well-meant phrase, said out of place,
Can cut me like a knife.
I know that I'm the one to blame,
I cause self-inflicted tension,
And I wish I didn't react that way,
But it's all done without intention.

I know I'm going to have to try to take
Those innocent words you say
For as genuine as they are
And not doubt the sentiment in any way.
My mind, it just seems to have
Too many flaws to mention,
But with your love I'm going to try to change,
And that will be done with FULL INTENTION.

We Can't Go Down This Road

Once again money is put before a broken soul,
Re-opening the cell to a shattered and fragile mind,
Convincing the vulnerable there is nothing more that can be done,
Their only safety net a seldom answered telephone line.

The walls once their protection has been demolished,
The vital communications line has been taken down.
People are left stranded in turmoil and dark confusion
Because there's not enough cash to go around.

When will we learn
You cannot put a price
On giving someone a semblance
Of a better life.

Helping people fight their demons
That they cannot fight alone.
How many lives will be lost before we realise
We can't go down this road?

With cutbacks and the economy
There is no doubt that money is tight,
But it's also wasted on peripheral things
And that cannot be right.

The route of progress costs and is essential,
But there is a fine line
Between forging forward to put a man on Mars
And dragging mental health support back twenty years in time.

When will we learn
We can't stand idly by.
We should be putting money into this
Instead of letting the stream of hope run dry.

We've come so far, we can't go back,
But once the seeds have been sown
There'll be no options – no second chances
So we can't go down this road.

The 'dead end' sign is ahead of us
And we can't go down this road.

Love By Any Other Name

Sometimes I see
Him in her,
Although I never realised
It at first.
Too busy grieving,
Trying to find my feet.
Not sure she could
Really make my life complete.
It's been five years now,
But how time has hurried,
And I understand now
I should never have worried,
Because I'm sure she's an angel
He sent to me,
So I could begin my life again,
Complete and happily.
Sometimes I see
Him in her,
Both ease the pain
And subdue the hurt.
She's so different to him
But sometimes just the same.
This is love
'By any other name'.

The Face of a Grief-stricken Man

He sat alone on the wooden bench,
Staring into space,
A shattered look of pain and loss
Written on his face.
So I sat beside him,
I wasn't sure if he knew I was there,
But he didn't need to say one word
To show how heavy the cross he had to bear.
The rain it softly began to fall,
And it was then his tears came.
It was as if nature were sharing
In this man's grief and pain.
And then he turned and looked at me,
And I gently took his trembling hand,
And I'll never forget the tragic face
Of that grief-stricken man.
I looked up to the Lord
And I questioned my belief,
Is there no heart so lonely
Than one in grief?
I could feel his heart breaking,
But what could I say?
Even if I could find the words,
They wouldn't take the hurt away.
So we sat there in silence
For how long, I didn't know,
But soon the dusk came rolling in
And storm clouds threatened to grow.
Then he whispered to me,
'It's time for you to go,
There must be somebody that's worrying
And waiting for you at home.'

And he told me 'Every day let the one you love
Know what they mean to you,
Because one day they will be gone
And it won't be me sitting here broken, but you,
Holding onto memories
That are just a passage written in time,
The end of her story,
And now the end of mine.'
Then he turned back,
Staring into space,
Images of yesterday
Replayed upon his face,
And as I walked away
I could not look back
Into the haunted face
Of a grief-stricken man.

Cry Out Silently

I was just a kid,
I was only ten,
Too young to understand
What was happening back then.
I was pretty new to life,
Wasn't sure how I was meant to feel,
And I believed them when they said
The monsters I saw were not real.
I thought everybody cried themselves to sleep,
I felt afraid, so I acted out.
If only they'd realised the gravity of it back then
And what it was really all about.

Just two years later,
My frustrated mind was consumed with rage,
But everybody brushed it off
And said it was just my age.
I started taking dangerous risks,
Crossed every kind of boundary,
Praying someone would figure out
That things weren't right with me.
The dark shadows gathered around me,
I watched helplessly as hope slipped away,
But I was still just a kid,
Who would believe what I wished I could say?

I am an adult now,
The monsters are still around.
The dark shadows still follow me,
Even when the sun goes down.
I did eventually find the courage to speak out
About what was going on,
But for me it was too late,
The damage had been done.
So don't underestimate a child's thoughts,
Don't let them be a missed opportunity – like me.
You need to look, not just listen for a voice,
Because they can only cry out silently.

Cornered

She was crying
In the corner.
Passing peers just laughed
Or ignored her.
Inside she was broken,
Her soul was crushed.
She surrendered,
Her spirit hushed.
A seed was sown
That would shape her life.
Her foundations would be built on words
Full of hate and spite.

And as she grew,
The bullying
Became her all,
Her everything.
Her confidence
All but gone.
Her self-esteem –
There was none.
She wasn't like the others
Who craved fame and glory.
All she wanted was just a kinder chapter
To her sad story.

She started to believe
What they'd say.
She had nothing else
Anyway.
And when she left school,
The damage was done
And would plague her life
For years to come.
Things said to her,
Years ago it seems,
Would pervade her thoughts
For eternity.

She really tried
To overcome her past,
But like brief, happy moments,
It didn't last.
Although sometimes her heart
With hope was filled,
It always came down to the rocky foundations
That she could not rebuild.
Now she still sits
Crying in the corner.
Nobody cares to look,
And she's relieved that they ignore her.

Then He is Yours Forever

My mind is so full of sadness, Lord,
I don't know which road I'll have to take.
Although one's a little further along in my story,
They both lead to heartache.

It's not the weight on my back, Lord,
That is such a heavy load
But the pain I carry in my heart
That makes me fear both these roads.

Just give me a little more time with him, Lord,
Just a bit more time together,
Because when the day comes that I lose him,
Then he is yours forever.

We've been part of each other's lives
For such a very long time.
I am half of his soul
And he is half of mine.

So just give me a chance to tell him how I feel, Lord,
Even though I've told him every day we've been together.
I just need to say it to him, one more time,
Then he's safely yours forever.

The Perfect In – Purrfect

Even my friends who love animals
Were at first a little wary of him.
His eyes don't exactly sit straight on his face,
And his 'normal' look can appear menacing.
But, in fact, that little multicoloured cat
Has the sweetest heart I have ever known.
He might look a little bit different, a little bit odd,
But he makes this old house of mine into the perfect home.

The dark reds and rusts amongst the golds
Camouflage the outline of his mouth,
Guests are never really sure if he's scowling or smiling.
His big amber eyes, when fixed, seem to follow you around,
And they're not sure if it's disturbing or beguiling.
I'm the first to admit his look is unusual, but isn't quirky 'in'?
And I just see a million unparalleled reasons to love that boy
Every time I take a look at him.

Sometimes he sticks his two teeth out,
It's the most precious thing I think I've ever seen,
Like two icicles hanging from a mossy rock,
Perhaps that's why people – at first – aren't so keen.
But he's the gentlest of gentlemen,
And the only thing he nibbles on with those teeth
Is the gourmet food he likes to dine on,
And sometimes when I'm in bed they kindly tickle my feet.

Sometimes I have to hold my laughter in
When people first visit me,
Because after they nervously steal a look at him,
He goes and sits right next to them, on the settee.
They gasp as he stares at them,
But as his gorgeous eyelashes flutter up and down,
In that second they fall under his spell,
He can always win anyone around.

All my friends – and now 'our' friends –
Are now all eager to visit me,
But of course, he's the centre of all the attention,
From 'Mr Not So Sure' to 'Mr Popularity'.
He might look a little curious,
He's definitely stand-alone,
But this perfect in – purrfect little boy
Makes this old house every one's perfect home.

Mine is the Story

The colour is draining
And turning to grey.
People don't even see
That I'm fading away.
As the memories diminish,
It's hurting because
Mine is the story
That never was.

All that I've lived for
And all that I've done
Wasn't really worth anything,
When it had never begun.
Why would anyone remember,
How could they even care,
If they have no memory
Of me being there?

There're no clues I was here,
There'll be no mark of the loss,
Because mine is the story
That never was.
Is it too late to change things?
Or have I already lost the game?
Is there no way to let people
Try and remember my name?

Can I still make a difference?
Or am I too far gone?
Will mine be the story
Remembered by none?
Maybe this wasn't the journey
I was meant to do.
Perhaps I wasn't noticed,
Because I was just passing through.

But at journey's end with my Lord,
I know I'll be someone.
He'll hold me gently and mine will be
The story just begun.

Those Who Know Most of All

It's not the celebrities who speak out that will change things,
Although they will give comfort to some.
It's not the lawmakers or the media
Who can reclaim what is going on.

It's the people who are living
With something that is not a choice,
Those who feel lost, who feel alone
And feel no one listens to their voice.

Some afraid to speak out
For fear of having any little support lost,
Scared to make a complaint
In case their lifeline is cut off.

The only way things will change
Is if we listen to their gentle call,
For they are those who know what needs to be done,
They're those who know most of all.

Those qualified and lettered to help,
Those knowledgeable and erudite
Need to know books don't tell the whole story,
And their conclusions aren't always right.

It's up to those in the profession to learn
Sometimes they need to put aside
All they've thought before.
Just listen – because in just a few words
Someone in trouble can explain it all.

Every single person needs to listen,
Encourage the weak voices to get strong
And to understand what doesn't always make sense
Doesn't automatically mean that it's wrong.

The opportunity is right in front of us,
We CAN break down that wall.
We can change this broken system
By hearing those who know most of all.

Half-leaving

She didn't try to whisper what she said to you,
You swallowed hard, your mouth was dry.
She didn't try to hide her spite towards you,
And I could see that you were trying not to cry.
I saw something in your face
Only another once-crushed soul would recognise,
The look of a fractured, broken spirit
And the total resignation in your eyes.

Are you half-leaving,
Half-willing to stay?
Don't tell me that you're not hurt
By the mean things that she says.
Do you think you still love her?
Because if that's what you believe,
There'll always be half of you that wants to stay
And half of you that wants to leave.

You're afraid to answer her back
When she's publicly so mean,
But I guess I understand
Why you don't argue with her
When she's so quick to cause a scene.
I get it more than you know,
I had the same kind of relationship with 'him'.
I was once in the position
That you now find yourself in.

I was half-leaving,
Half-willing to stay.
It took all the courage I could find
To finally get away.
It certainly wasn't easy,
but it's left me truly believing
I made the right decision
when I wasn't just half-leaving.

The Secret Hollow

Somewhere in the woods,
In a hollow, I hid a secret.
I couldn't tell you it,
Because I knew you wouldn't keep it.

You ask why I secreted it
In an old, aged tree,
And I tell you, it's because I knew
The woods would not judge me.

But now time has matured you and I accept your trust,
So I'll tell you which trail to follow
So you can read my secret
That's hidden in the hollow.

Somewhere in the woods,
Entrusted to a tree that's tall and old,
Is the biggest secret
That I have never told.

The secret is not so important
As it was before.
So I don't need the aged tree
To hide it any more.

The woods hold many secrets
From when to them I've spoken freely,
Secrets I know they won't tell,
Kept by each and every tree.

The woods' beasts have probably seen it
Before you even reach it.
So I guess, in a way,
It was never really a secret.

Did you find it?
Find the right trail to follow?
Was the secret still inside
That tree's small, jagged hollow?

You look surprised –
What have you got to say?
You found the secret,
But the elements have washed the words away.

I Don't Want to Build Castles Any More

She sat enveloped in the sand, in her little red shorts
And fringed hat with her blue bucket and spade.
Every parent on the beach turned to look
When she squealed 'Mommy and Daddy,
look at the castle that I made.'

Her older brother heard her too
And did what older brothers do.
He stood up and turned around
Then ran and kicked her castle down.

She started crying loudly 'Look what he's done!'
Daddy shouted at him, followed by an angry Mom.
She angrily added 'That was so spiteful.
What did you do that for?'
As his little sister lapped up the fuss and wailed

'I don't want to build castles any more!'
When she was sixteen, she met a boy,
They soon had a baby on the way.
Her boyfriend talked about finding them a wonderful home,
But until the baby came, with her parents they'd stay.

He had big hopes,
He had big dreams.
His hard work paid off – so it seems.

He rented them a flat,
He was so excited,
But his young bride,
She was not so delighted.

He said 'This will be our castle,
And I will be the king,
And for you – the queen –
I'd do anything.'

He constantly talked about their
baby girl and their new home,
In fact, he talked of nothing else.
He often asked her 'Tell me what you need,
So we can make this home a castle for ourselves.'

This time she didn't revel in his attention
Or his constant fuss.
She thought of saying 'It seems this castle
Is for you and not for us.'

Then one day she said 'I don't want to build castles any more,
It would just be crushed, like before.'
She'd been so nervous about being a mother to his baby,
Or was she falling out of love with him, maybe.

He did all he could to cheer her up,
But even at his young age, it wouldn't be enough.
They had lost their love along the way,
And he couldn't find the right words to say.

Since the baby had arrived,
Life had been so tough,
Both felt they were too young
And didn't know enough.

She couldn't settle in the home that they'd made,
It took her back twelve years to her bucket and spade.
When all that was lost was a castle of sand,
She knew she had so much to lose, but he didn't understand.

Her parents helped out
Whenever they could.
His parents too
Were so good.

When they split, she was devastated,
Emotions she had not anticipated.
He visited their daughter every day
And offered plans for a family holiday.

A week on the beach was what they both needed,
And their daughter sat enveloped in the sand
with her bucket and spade,
And when she shouted, every parent looked around,
'Mommy, Daddy, look at the castle I made.'

A flicker of recognition on both their faces
As they thought about their own past,
they were still quite young,
When she had been the one building castles,
And he was an older brother trying to act
like he was smart and strong.

Then he gently kissed his ex-girlfriend and said
'I will do what it takes,
If you give me a chance to take things a lot slower
And to correct any of my mistakes.'

She kissed him back and said to him
'There are no mistakes that you made.
We just need to take things slowly,
We both rushed into everything, and I got afraid.'

He said 'I know you don't
Want to build castles any more,
But what about a HOME for our little girl,
Whom we both adore?

'And if she can build
A castle of sand,
Then we can build back the love
And the future for our family that we once planned.'

All Changed Now

His downcast eyes are weary
As he still walks the paths,
Six thirty in the morning
As early shadows are cast.
He walks the hills,
Keeps to the route they kept
From when his best friend was by his side,
He follows in their old footsteps.

But it's all changed now,
He walks those roads alone.
Time took his best friend,
And now he's on his own.
He knows that he's grieving,
But he's not chasing a ghost.
It's just the memories of where they spent their time
Keep him and his precious boy feeling close.

The gathering winds around him seem to whisper,
Telling his old boy to heel,
And as they rustled through the reeds, he's sure he can see
His precious dog running through the fields.
He tightly cradles the lead in his coat pocket
As he walks down the dusty tracks,
Sad in knowing no amount of wishing
Will bring his best friend back.

The cool air is getting colder now,
And it blows harshly on his face,
And he wonders how this beautiful landscape
Could be such a lonely place.
He knows it's all changed now,
And no matter how hard he prays,
He's all alone through long, long nights
And solitary companionless days.

Six thirty in the morning,
Another day of walking their route alone,
And now he waits for the day, at the end of the line,
When his best friend will come to walk HIM home.

Clinging to the Corners of a Circle

I'm clinging to the corners of a circle,
I'm trying to light a match under the sea.
I want to make a bed out of a single cotton thread,
I lie awake so that I can sleep soundly.
Everything I'm trying to do seems impossible,
I'm shouting too loud for anyone to hear my pleas,
I'm clinging to the corners of a circle,
Standing on tiptoe whilst I'm down on my knees.
I'm skating on an unfrozen river,
I'm trying to harvest diamonds from the grain.
I'm standing in the middle of the railroad tracks,
Holding up tissue paper to stop a speeding train.
I've come in disguise, as myself,
I'm rooted to the ground as away I fly,
And when I look at you, I swear to tell the truth,
And I promise you it will be an outright lie.
I'm trying to climb a ladder that has no rungs,
I'm building a picket fence to stop a flood.
I'm building a house without foundations,
I'm doing bad things because I'm good.
I' m descending UP a tall mountain,
I'm walking level on all its inclines.
I'm clinging to the corners of a circle,
Hopelessly lost within its parallel lines.

Amelie

Honey-gold with amber eyes, so mystical, so seductive.
They draw you in – then push you out –
they won't reveal the secrets of her soul.
Her fine, soft fur, the patina of an aged oak wood,
Soft reds and creams wrapped in shades of gold.

And when she leaps before a cinnamon sun
Flies loose that soft fur,
And as it catches the sun's golden rays,
It looks like little red angels falling to earth.

She watches me – but I dare only glance,
Her eyes quizzical, curious – knowing,
I want to fall into those amber pools of light,
So warm, so comforting, like a late-night bonfire glowing.

She walks towards me with the poise and grace of a dancer,
Each foot purposely laid down in a well-thought place,
The choreography of the cat, so mathematical,
yet so uncommitted,
A discerning, strong look on such a fragile, beautiful face.

Sublime stretching that in itself is a work of art,
And as she jumps on a whisper of wind,
her body is a sculptor's dream.
She lands so quietly, so softly, so perfectly,
You wouldn't know she was there if you hadn't seen.

She moulds herself into my lap,
So carefully, so sure.
Gentle purr resonates,
Strong, calming and pure.

My soul yearns for this complicated creature,
This intelligent, intricate puzzle of feline,
This kaleidoscope of crazy and amazing,
Whose heart she's thankfully nestled in is mine.

The Butterfly

I feel the touch of a butterfly's wing,
And I'm sure it was you,
Assuring me you're always here with me,
To guide and help me through.

Now I see the white butterfly dancing with a friend
On the temperate breeze,
And I watch as they fly together,
Past the terracotta sun and into the trees.

And I wish that I was a butterfly,
So I could join you in flight,
Because losing you was devastating,
And I miss you in my life.

I watch as the butterflies come and go,
But I know which is you.
Are the others souls I've lost,
To comfort and protect me too?

This world is so hard without you,
No one understands me like you did,
Who truly accepted me and loved me
As an adult, as a kid.

But it seems only right
A beautiful butterfly would be you,
Free at last and out of pain,
I just wish I was a butterfly too.

That Bully

In the gym changing rooms, she sits crying,
Everyone else has long since gone.
She's still in her shorts and her tee shirt,
The old tarnished hook still has her warm clothes hanging on.

Her head is buried in her folded arms
That lie across her trembling knees,
Sobbing so deeply it echoes all around the room
And tells the story of how terrified she is.

For a second she looks up and sees me watching her,
Her haunted eyes pleading with me to help her out somehow.
She doesn't say a word, but she doesn't need to,
You can see her barely hanging on right now.

That bully has crushed her to nothing,
And that cold room seems to resonate her pain.
I was once in the hell that she is in now,
And it unnervingly brings it back to me again.

I remember sitting, hurting, crying in the playground,
As that bully rolled off mean and cruel things to me.
I know how it feels to have your soul broken,
She's in the dark place I once used to be.

I had no allies, no protection,
No willing friends to understand.
So for years that bully had free rein
To stamp my self-esteem into the ground.

Now I'm looking into the eyes of that young girl,
She's a mirror image of my once broken reflection.
It's like going back in time to when it was me,
We have this sad connection.

I smile at her understandingly then walk away,
I glance back, her fear so palpable, so clear to see,
But she and I know her torment is far from over
Because that bully who terrorises her – IS ME.

Time I Let You In

For him my heart still weeps,
For him my heart still aches.
So this is a step I never thought
That I would ever take.
To let my fragile guard down,
To work cautiously to being sure
That I could share my heart with you,
To try and love once more.

The infinite bond I share with him
Is forever unbreakable.
The love I'll always have for him
Is truly unmistakeable.
There's a place in my heart
That's reserved just for him,
But I realise now there's space for you,
And it's time I let you in.

I've been fighting with my conscience,
My soul's been broken since he's gone,
But if I could choose a new best friend
Then you would be the one.
People say our lives are just like chapters in a book,
And sometimes new ones have to begin,
So I need to be on the very first page,
So I can let you in.

I'm still getting to know you,
You're still getting to know me,
But when we met the very first time,
You seemed to know immediately.
I admit it's taken me a long time
To trust the feelings that have set in,
But now I have no doubt that I love you,
I'm so blessed to let you in.

A Shoulder to Cry On

Hiding from my demons,
My life a living hell.
Still, everybody said to me,
I'd never looked so well.
So I just smiled and thanked them,
It was too hard to explain
This dirty little secret
They would never believe anyway.

I was always the listener,
They always came to me.
They thought I had all the answers –
How's that for irony!
But I would never let anyone down,
And it felt good to help people out.
For that time I could conceal the real me
That no one knew about.

So I'd paint a smile on my face
And fool everyone,
But when was home all by myself,
I'd wish I had a shoulder to cry on.
But I am only one of many
Who feel the truth they need to hide,
Who yearn for validation
And a reassuring hug sometimes.

People think I'm the strong one,
Confident all the time,
But they couldn't be more wrong,
They have no idea of the constant battles in my mind.
A little of my soul is lost each day,
A little more hope is gone,
And I'M the one who desperately needs
A shoulder to cry on.

I Recognise His Face

You can see him wandering through my dreams,
You can always find him there,
Different times, different places, different landscapes,
He's in every sweet vision, every scary nightmare.
A dream would just not be complete
If each moment he didn't grace,
I don't know who he is,
But I recognise his face.

Maybe he's an angel,
A familiar comfort that's mine to keep,
Walking with me through minds bizarre,
Protecting me whilst I sleep.
For whatever reason he is there,
He always leaves a lasting trace,
I've met him and I can't forget him,
Because I recognise his face.

Is he my soulmate,
My best friend or my brother?
How is it we have never met,
Yet he touches me like no other.
And when I close my eyes at night,
He will take his place,
And I thank God I'll have no fear of the dark,
Because I'll recognise his face.

Another Man's Word

He walked with an old, weather-beaten cane,
An uneven scar knitted across his face.
He had long, grey, rambling hair,
And he lived in a big, old, scary place.

People would cross the road
When they saw him on the street.
The kids would run away and hide,
Quickened hearts but even faster feet.

Nobody really knew him,
So they lived on stories they had heard.
Each year the tales got more bizarre,
One man judged on another man's word.

He became a local legend, of sorts,
But not in a favourable way at all,
And the adults began to believe in what they said,
Stoking the fire and adding the fuel.

Then one day, a new family arrived in town,
And their little girl was playing in the street
When she heard someone approaching her,
His cane clicking on the pavement as he shuffled his feet.

Her new friends took to their heels
And screamed at her to run,
But she hadn't heard all the town's stories
And wasn't sure what they were running from.

As he got within a foot, she said 'Hello,'
She had no reason to be afraid.
Sometimes it takes an innocent soul
For a difference to be made.

He looked up, scowling, but saw her smile
That extended to her eyes,
And to everyone's amazement, he smiled back,
It had taken a small child to shame the 'wise'?

People began to fill the pavement,
And in a gentle voice he said 'Hello' to them all.
The children gathered around and asked about his scar,
Suddenly to them, he didn't seem like a monster any more.

Now people walk the pavement with him,
But a few stories still remain,
And he likes that there's still a little mystery to him,
That no one can explain.

Finally, he was included as part of the town,
And he now never walks that road alone,
His hair is still grey and rambling,
And to the kids delight, he still lives in a big, old, scary home.

The Secret House

At the back of those old playing fields,
Beyond the long, overgrown grass,
A broken fence, a gateway to our secret place,
A once loved, now rundown old house.
It was such a big part of my life,
When I had just turned ten,
That I only have to close my eyes now
And I'm right back there again.

My three best friends and I would gather
At the red telephone box across the road,
Firstly, making sure we had our stories straight
For a fictional 'where we'd been' when we got home.
We knew we'd be in big trouble
If we told our parents where we'd played,
But we were well practised in telling little white lies,
Even at that tender age.

That old, broken-down house
Had meant so much to us
That even with an old broom we found we'd cleaned around,
Although we were only really pushing around the dust.
And when it rained, we'd grab our wooden fruit box seats,
Quickly go and sit in the corner of the room.
The roof had a gap that had in turn
cracked the ceilings below it,
So we'd just sit there chatting whilst
the rain came falling through.

We never ventured up the stairs,
The handrail was on the floor, the steps slightly out of place.
It seems funny how at that young age
We still had a sense of keeping ourselves safe.
That old house held all of our secrets,
Saw our tears, arguments and friendships grow.
It was the place our personalities were shaped,
Forever sewn into the fabric of our lives,
Our amazing, secret home.

Then came the day we never saw coming,
Something terrible that had never crossed our young minds.
Our treasured secret friend was being pulled down,
And we saw the remnants of our young lives
broken up in the skip outside.
I don't know how long it was we stood there,
Our tears falling quickly and silently,
And when we couldn't bear to watch it any more,
We ran home with a burning pain in our tummies.

The next day, we all got there early,
Unsure of what we would find,
But beyond, our worst fears were realised,
Our house was gone and dust was all that was left behind.
There was nothing left for us to do but leave,
Pain in our hearts, knowing our special place was gone for good,
But even now I believe there's a little part of us
In the magical place where our secret house once stood.

Shadows on the Wall

He would sit for hours
When he and his kid sister were small,
Making all kinds of shapes
Into shadows on the wall.
He would use his hands to make
Giraffes, birds and aeroplanes,
Whilst his little sister giggled and laughed
At those innocent childhood games.

But time, it passed so quickly,
And soon they both were grown.
He was a proud, young, married man,
Now with children of his own.
And when all three kids were old enough,
He sat and taught them all
How to make whatever they wanted
Into shadows on the wall.

Times were changing quickly,
And as a soldier, he got the call,
Summoned to take his place
And try and win a war.
He walked with his brothers
To a place of no return,
Then, alone he was settled at a simple guardhouse
With some harsh lessons, quick to learn.

Every day he would guard with his gun,
A little afraid that he was on his own.
His thoughts were of his young family,
And he prayed he'd soon be home.
Each time the sun began to set,
The childhood games he would recall,
But now gone were the silhouettes of innocence,
He now feared the shadows on the guardhouse wall.

Soon the allies took the upper hand,
Hopes were high it would end this war,
But not before one more soul
Would pay the ultimate price of all.
Shot, he lay in the guardhouse, dying,
The last soldier to fall,
Watching his life ebb away
As a shadow on the wall.

As his eyes finally closed,
There was something he never saw,
His broken body, wrapped in the wings of an angel,
Ascending in the shadows on the wall.

Love You as Much as Him

Why can't I love you
As much as I loved him?
When can our story
Of two souls as one begin?
Am I just afraid
That I will lose you too?
Is that the reason
I can't get close to you?

You're so different to him,
But in many ways you're just the same.
I know my heart wants to hold you,
But I couldn't bear to lose again.
I hope you don't realise
The turmoil that I'm in,
Because I really want to
Love you as much as I loved him.

The pain of losing him
Was the worst I've ever known,
So did I rush into meeting you
For the fear of being alone?
I quickly found you
And I took you in,
I thought it would be easy to love you straight away,
Just as much as I loved him.

They say that time is a great healer,
But it doesn't change the fact
That he is gone forever,
And he's never coming back.
I have no choice but to ride the wave,
Then maybe some day
I could love you as much as him,
Just in a different way.

He'll always be my always and forever,
And not even time can take that away.
I thought that we would always be together,
And it's so hard to understand that my life has changed.
But I guess I need to accept
This different world that I'm now in,
And one day I hope to love you
As much as I'll ALWAYS love him.

Captive

Sleep
Offers no relief.
The quietude of the darkness
Affords me no comfort, no peace.
Not even the rain,
On whom I can always depend,
Can dampen this anguish,
My dear, faithful friend.
I see you but can't hear you,
The silence is so loud,
My mind taken captive
By a different kind of cloud.
Then through the miasma
A bird's early call,
Is this the salvation
That I've been praying for?
But through the fog that has settled on my mind
The bird's refrain sounds so wrong,
More a lonesome portent
Than a sweet morning birdsong.
This bed more a prison
Than my wonted sanctuary,
And I pray time will be forgiving,
Be gracious and set me free.

FÜR AUTOREN A HEART FOR AUTHORS À L'ÉCOUTE DES AUTEURS MIA KAPΔIA ΓIA ΣΥ
FÖR FÖRFATTARE UN CORAZÓN POR LOS AUTORES YAZARLARIMIZA GÖNÜL VERELIM
PER AUTORI ET HJERTE FOR FORFATTERE EEN HART VOOR SCHRIJVERS TEMOS OS Aι
SZÍNKÉRT SERCE DLA AUTORÓW EIN HERZ FÜR AUTOREN A HEART FOR AUTHORS À L'ÉC
BCEЙ ДУШОЙ К АВТОРАМ ETT HJÄRTA FÖR FÖRFATTARE À LA ESCUCHA DE LOS AL
MIA KAPΔIA ΓIA ΣYΓΓΡΑΦΕΙΣ UN CUORE PER AUTORI ET HJERTE FOR FORFATTERE E
LARIMIZA   ZÖINKÉRT SERCE DLA AUTORÓW EIN HERZ
SCHRIJVERS   OS O   AÇÃO BCEЙ ДУШОЙ К АВТОРАМ ETT HJÄRTA

The author

Diane Valerie Burgess was born in Birmingham
in 1970. She has worked at British Rail, the
Birmingham Heartlands Hospital and is the lead
vocalist in a Carpenters tribute band.
At twenty-seven, Diane was diagnosed with severe
rheumatoid arthritis, which caused her right hand
to become deformed, and in 2021, she suffered
a stroke, which paralysed her left hand. Despite
this, Diane is still able to write poetry, her favourite
pastime. In September 2022, Diane's life took on a
new direction when married the first man she has
ever loved.

FORFATTERE EEN HART VOOR SCHRIJ **novum 📖 PUBLISHER FOR NEW AUTHORS**
EIN HERZ FÜR AUTOREN A HEART FOR
T HJÄRTA FÖR FÖRFATTARE A LA ESCUCHA DE LOS AUTORES YAZARLARIMIZA
N CUORE PER AUTORI ET HJERTE FOR ORFATTERE EEN HART VOOR SCHRIJVERS
T SZERZŐINKÉRT SERCE DLA AUTORÓW EIN HERZ FÜR AUTOREN A HEART FOR AUTH
O CORAÇÃO BCEЙ ДУШОЙ K ABTOPAM ET HJÄRTA FÖR FÖRFATTARE UN CORAZÓN
DES AUTEURS MIA   ORI ET HJERTE FOR FO
YAZARLARIMIZA G   SERCE DLA AUTORÓW EIN H

The publisher

*He who stops
getting better
stops being good.*

This is the motto of novum publishing, and our focus
is on finding new manuscripts, publishing them and
offering long-term support to the authors.
Our publishing house was founded in 1997, and since
then it has become THE expert for new authors and
has won numerous awards.

**Our editorial team will peruse each manuscript
within a few weeks free of charge and without
obligation.**

You will find more information about
novum publishing and our books on the internet:

w w w . n o v u m - p u b l i s h i n g . c o . u k

novum PUBLISHER FOR NEW AUTHORS

Rate
this book
on our
website!

www.novum-publishing.co.uk

Printed in Great Britain
by Amazon

25557058R00101